Savor a l

LEADERSHIP MINTS

**101 Ways To Freshen
Your Feeling For Leading**

By Peter Jeff

Take a 5-Minute Leadership Mints Break

You're busy. Too busy to attend as many seminars and workshops on leadership as you might like and too busy to keep up with so many books and blogs on leadership thinking.

Relax, take a deep breath and savor Leadership Mints, 101 bite-sized ideas to recharge your leadership batteries.

Consumed like a breath mint —quick and on-the-go—*Leadership Mints* is a breath of fresh air filled with 101 short stories that personalize leadership principles and emotional behaviors.

Like its candy counterpart, a Leadership Mint is easily spooned, quickly digested and immediately satisfying. Most of the content-rich, principle-centered, ImproveMINT-oriented stories can be read in less than 5 minutes.

Many leaders find it convenient and productive to conduct a *5-Minute Leadership Mints Break* as part of their regular staff meetings to freshen their team's leadership thinking on 16 different leadership competencies.

LEADERSHIP MINTS PUBLISHING

Grand Rapids, Michigan
www.LeadershipMints.com

@LeaderMintsGuy

ISBN- 978-0615936970

Second Printing

© 2015, Peter Jeff

Leadership Development
Simple & Quick

The leader's primary role is to develop other leaders, according to the prevailing leadership development research, studies and surveys. Yet studies show that leaders developing others leaders ranks 4th from the bottom in the amount of time leaders actually spend on formal leadership development programs, according to the Leadership 2012 Study Focusing on Trends and Best Practices conducted by Corporate University Xchange, (CorpU) - a global learning and leadership research firm. That's why:

1. *Leadership Mints* is specifically designed –Simply-- as a tool to help busy leaders develop other leaders—Quickly. In 5-minute learning modules.

2. *Leadership Mints* capitalizes on the trend in the leadership development industry toward on-going, integrated, on-the-job experiential study of leadership rather than a series of separately scheduled leadership seminars or workshops.

3. *Leadership Mints* fills a key learning gap especially for newly minted leaders and their busy coaches and mentors: the need for a time-sensitive, weekly reminder of key concepts that could stand on its own or be used as a formal follow-up to a workshop or seminar.

4. **Leadership Mints** broadens the scope of leadership development for all busy employees coping with on-going change while doing more with less—not merely those who have been appointed leaders.

CONTENTS

(See chapter by chapter Table of Contents 272-276)

QUICK START, 10-15
Your Owner's Manual to Leadership Mints

INTRODUCTION, 11

EXTRA BONUS MINTS

INTRODUCTION

What's a Leadership Mint?

Short stories read in 5 minutes or less that personalize leadership principles. That's a Leadership Mint. Freshen your bottom-line thinking. On-the-go. Quickly. Easily. Daily. Like its candy counterpart, a Leadership Mint is easily spooned, quickly digested and immediately accessible. Invest a few minutes of reading for a lifetime of leading. The time it takes to read a Leadership Mint story is posted beneath each headline to remind you how quickly you can freshen your leadership breath & breadth and enhance your EQ in an IQ world.

You can digest any one of the 101 Leadership Mints in any order very easily. You can read two pages at a time –the length of most of the 101 stories. The book is designed so that you can glean enough information or inspiration in 5 minutes reading time to more effectively lead on a specific issue. Need help reprimanding others? *(Mint 55)*. Need help fending off your critics? *(Mint 62)*. Need help convincing others? *(Mint 65)*. Need help focusing? *(Mint 70)*.

ImproveMINTS

Each Leadership Mint ends with an *ImproveMINT:* a one-sentence, call-to-action summary that reinforces the intended key learning of the story. For a list of all 101 *ImproveMINTS*, see pages 264-267. Need something more situational? See the Leadership Mints Owner's Manual (pages 10-15). Need something more behavioral –from attitude to strategic thinking, see pages 268-271. Need something even more specific, see the 7-page Index beginning on page 279.

Who Should Read
Leadership Mints?

Busy people. *Leadership Mints* is designed for busy people at all levels regardless of your leadership experience.

- If you're a seasoned leader, *Leadership Mints* is a **Refresher** tool to share with others.
- If you're a newly-minted leader, *Leadership Mints* **Reinforces** what you have learned but not yet practiced enough on the job.
- If you are a first-time leader or would-be leader, *Leadership Mints* **Reassures** your self-confidence in applying leadership principles and complements your participation in leadership seminars and workshops.

Concise and to the point, *Leadership Mints* are often served at staff meetings and team meetings. Many team leaders purchase multiple copies of *Leadership Mints* to share like the candy mint variety and freshen their staff's thinking on issues ranging from gaining trust *(Mint 44)* to partnering with others *(Mint 49)* to teaching the value of diversity *(Mint 57)*.

Take a 5-Minute
Leadership Mints Break

Some leaders conduct a *5-Minute Leadership Mints Break* during their staff meetings as a non-threatening, teaching opportunity that sharpens current leaders and shapes future leaders in three distinct competencies: **Creating** *(Mints 1-34)*; **Collaborating** *(Mints 35-66)* and **Communicating** *(Mints 67-101)*. The team leader rotates the Leadership Mints Break Discussion Leader's Role to each member of his or her staff a week in advance of the staff meeting. Then at the next staff meeting, the designated Leadership Mints Break Discussion Leader facilitates a

5-minute learning session on one of the 101 stories personalizing leadership principles. See the *Owner's Manual* to Leadership Mints (pages 10-15) for a quick start to using Leadership Mints as a leadership development tool. Review the 17 different situations or challenges your team may be facing and the specific Mints that address those issues. Turn to page 286 to learn how to lead your own 5-Minute Leadership Mint Break at your next staff meeting.

Facilitating Feedback

Many leaders leverage the lessons learned during the 5-Minute Leadership Mints Break to facilitate on-going feedback with their direct reports. Surveys show the lack of regular feedback is the top complaint employees lodge when they look for greener pastures. You'd like to invest more time into grooming your staff with regular feedback and concerned coaching. But when you are putting out so many fires every day who has time for fire prevention? Consider this book your fire prevention kit to keep your staff sparking with ideas and ideals without burning them or yourself out. Using this fire prevention kit for five minutes at weekly staff meetings, you and your staff will no longer dread the annual review process that is so often irrelevant and/or distorted by the time you and your staff members look back over the last 12 months (or more).

Now in savoring a *Leadership Mint* together during regular staff meetings, you and your direct reports will freshen your bottom-line thinking, your feeling for leading and leverage the value of on-going feedback in real time. All leaders know that employees join a company but they leave YOU—their leader, their boss—not the company. As the leader, only you can stop that brain drain. Only you can prevent those fires with this book. Sprinkled with provocative headlines, *Leadership Mints* is not your father's (or mother's) leadership book. These 101 stories are designed to spark a creative discussion and critical reflection on leadership behavior with stirring titles like these: *Slipping Into the Girdle of Innovation (Mint 13)* Leaders Are Great Kissers *(Mint 35) and Confessions of a Listener: Father I Have Sinned (Mint 67).* The 101 stories complement competency-based leadership development training programs that focus on issues from: Conflict Management (*Mint 55 Get Off Your Buts) to* Connecting with an Audience (*Mint 81 Public Speaking in a Bathrobe & Beyond) to* Writing Effective and Timely Status Reports *(Mint 93 Catching the 5:15 Train of Thought.)*

You'll also savor a few *Leadership Mints* packaged with an entertaining flair to relax you and maybe even trigger a smile as you refresh your leadership thinking on a key leadership principle. You'll enjoy "wine" at a Monday morning staff meeting *(Mint 9).* You'll color Easter eggs in a Leadership Talent Review meeting *(Mint 57).* You'll color with crayons like a kid again on butcher block paper in the executive conference room *(Mint 10).* And you'll savor other *Leadership Mints* flavored with TV personalities of yesteryear – from Fred Flintstone *(Mint 4)* to Jackie Gleason (*Mint 49)* to Eddie Haskell of *Leave It to Beaver* Fame *(Mint 60)* to Lt. Columbo *(Mint 82).*

Jack Nicklaus Invokes the "F" Word

Meanwhile you'll also savor *Leadership Mints* that refresh your thinking on the value of emotional intelligence and the significance of self-aware, caring and sharing leaders. They connect with others authentically. They consistently express their humanity with humility. And you'll also gain a rare behind-the-scenes exclusive look and appreciation for the emotional intelligence of Jack Nicklaus, professional golf's greatest player. Off the course, Nicklaus taught the author a lesson in personal leadership and authentic feeling that will surprise you. The Jack Nicklaus story *"On Fatherhood"* (page 173) is one of the Bonus Stories that follow each of three segments in *Leadership Mints.* In the first Bonus Mint in Part I CREATING (page 88), you'll learn how values-based leadership engages employees in creative problem-solving.   In the last Bonus Mint in Part III COMMUNICATING (page 257), you'll learn how to end a speech with pizzazz without saying the expected and therefore more perfunctory "Thank you."

ImproveMINTS Icon

To help you more fully process the feeling and the key take-away learning, each *Leadership Mint* vignette ends with *"Today's ImproveMINT"* – a summary one-liner that reminds you what you can do TODAY to "keep your leadership thinking in mint condition." The ***ImproveMINT*** is formatted at the end of each Leadership Mint and accentuated with a large candy-mint-like circular icon, like this:

Today's ImproveMINT

Savor at least one Leadership Mint a day
to keep your leadership thinking in mint condition.

Let's Get Started: It's easy to get started savoring ***Leadership Mints.*** You can read this book *:*

1. Specifically: (See Owner's Manual pages 10-15)
2. Behaviorally: according to 16 different leadership behaviors. (See pages 268-271)
3. Sequentially, randomly or topically in three defined segments:
   - Part I *Creativity*   (Mints   1-34)
   - Part II *Collaborating* (Mints 35-66)
   - Part III *Communicating* (Mints 67-101)

QUICK START

Your Owner's Manual
To Leadership Mints

Here's a quick-start to using *LEADERSHIP MINTS* as a professional development tool either collectively with your team or individually as a catalyst for your values-based leadership development. Use this Owner's Manual on the following five pages to better grasp a more strategic understanding and application of leadership principles. Think of this as a Table of Context more than a table of contents. Then follow these steps:

1. Find a specific situation facing you or team on the following alphabetical list of 17 different situations.
2. Review the descriptions of Mints (short stories) by number that reference that situation.
3. Turn to that specific Leadership Mint story for a 5-minute reading that spawns a discussion.
4. Reflect on the ImproveMINT that concludes each Leadership Mint with a key take-away learning, insight or understanding. Then discuss with your team how that learning can be applied to your specific situation.

In reviewing the Owner's Manual, consider yourself a values based leader who "takes the time to discover and reflect on what is most important to them," observes Northwestern University professor Harry Kraemer Jr. in his book *From Values to Action*. Values-based leaders leverage their EQ — their Emotional Quotient. They develop empathy for others and the social skillset to work together with others. They parlay a heightened sense of self-awareness—of knowing what they are feeling and how others are feeling towards them. And they develop their sense of composure to more readily self-regulate in challenging situations like these:

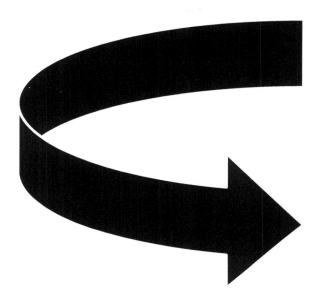

Table of Context

ALIGNING

Your team's effectiveness has slowed. The once smooth road to success has turned into a dusty and bumpy grind. Maybe it's time to DESIGNate more than deleGATE *(Mint 41)*. Leverage the introverts. *(Mint 57)*. Link the inherent interest and skills of the available talent FOR the job *(Mint 42)*. Celebrate the differences in your staff's behavioral preferences. Think of them as different birds and feed those birds differently *(Mint 58)*: eagles need results; peacocks need social interaction; doves need assurance and owls need details.

ATTITUDE

Your team's get-up-and-go got up and went. Flee the ennui. Turn up the music *(Mint 31)*. Laugh at yourself *(Mint 17)*. Hone your sense of humor *(Mint 18)*. Become more vulnerable *(Mint 51)* and beware of being too good to get better *(Mint 22)*. Be interested in others to get over your perceived shortcomings. *(Mint 21)*

COLLABORATING

It takes two to tango but your team seems to be stepping all over each other's feet. Maybe it's time that your staff saw themselves more systematically. Leverage your Navel Intelligence *(Mint 43)*. Celebrate complementary relationships where partners fill each other's gaps *(Mint 45)*. Learn from each other immediately after a project (*Mint 48*). And credit each other especially those standing in the shadows of others (*Mint 49*).

COMMUNICATING

The more you preach the less they seem to listen. Illustrate your message with a more passionate persistence (*Mint 77*) and graphic illustration (*Mint 85)*. Inspire with stories *(Mint 5)*. Gain greater understanding with analogy to explain complicated issues *(Mint 78)*. Compare with metaphors *(Mint 79)* Characterize with labels (*Mint 80)*. And codify with business cards *(Mint 91)*.

CONFLICT

Your team is screwing up and you seem to make matters worse. Resist derogatory remarks *(Mint 38)*. Get off your buts! Say "and" more often not "but" *(Mint 55)*. Validate the tense situation others are facing *(Mint 46*). Maintain self-control (*Mint 63)*. Cope with criticism *(Mint 62*). Apologize in writing (*Mint 92*). Thwart false praise (*Mint 60*). SCORE more than get sore *(Mint 64)*. And give 'em the VIP Treatment (*Bonus story, pages 88-99*).

CREATIVITY

Your team is tasked to do more with less. Stop to smell the ROSE of creativity *(Mint 20)*. Clear the slate *(Mint 33)* before you cross over the borders of your ImagiNATION *(Mint 11)*. Ride the RODEO *(Mint 12)* of creativity. Brainstorm new options (*Mint 32)*. Reach out high and away from it all *(Mint 29)*. Color your options (Mint 10). Innovate with new resources *(Mint 13)*.

Substitute for waning resources *(Mint 14)*. Repurpose existing resources *(Mint 30)*. And unleash hidden resources *(Mint 27)*.

ENGAGING

You have a new team. Now what? Get to know your team personally *(Mint 52)*. Respect them as individuals *(Mint 36)*. Trust them first *(Mint 53)*. Foster faith in them *(Mint 50)*. Climb down from your Ivory Tower *(Mint 66)*.

HUMILITY

You and your team have enjoyed enormous success. Stay grounded especially when others want to shine a spotlight on you.   See *Bonus Mint, pages 173-179* on golf legend Jack Nicklaus. Dare to be humble *(Mint 54)*. Keep your ego in check *(Mint 61)*. Beware of looking too polished *(Mint 82)*. Main self-control (*Mint 63*).

LISTENING

You and your team seem to do a lot of talking AT each other but very little listening with each other. Shut up and pucker up. Listen like a great kisser with focused attention and intention *(Mint 35)*. Listen with your eyes *(Mint 69)*. Beware of jumping to conclusions *(Mint 68)*. Realize that what they hear isn't always what you thought was said *(Mint 89)*. And so at times you may have to ask for forgiveness: Confessions of a Listener: Father, I Have Sinned *(Mint 67)*.

MEETINGS

Become the master of ceremonies to spice up your meetings *(Mint 94)* with snazzy introductions *(Mint 95)*. Visually connect with your audience before the meeting starts *(Mint 81)*. And make your meetings POP with a Premise and a Purpose *(Mint 96)*.

PERFORMANCE

You and your team have hit a rough patch and now you're spinning your wheels. Remind your team of the significance of their individual contribution to the organization *(Mint 4)*. Exaggerate effort to break through inertia with persistence *(Mint 77)*. Leverage the energizing aspect of change *(Mint 86)*. Accelerate quickly in launching a new project *(Mint 34)* and prepare weekly status reports that spark continued improvement and progress *(Mint 93)*.

PERSPECTIVE

You and you team are in a rut facing the same challenges in the same way. Remind your staff that where you stand on an issue depends on where you sit *(Mint 16)*. Break out of your individual Perception Prison *(Mint 15)*. Reverse the angle that you usually look at a challenge *(Mint 6)*. Beware of overlooking facts that are hidden in the open *(Mint 19)*. Narrow your attention span *(Mint 26)*. And reframe the issue *(Mint 8)*.

PERSUASION

You and your team are brimming with ideas yet no one can agree on a single idea. Play your ACE of compatibility first (Mint 40) then Pump LIFE into your proposals *(Mint 65)*. Revise your ideas *(Mint 87)* so they flow into the ideas of others *(Mint 75)*.

PROBLEM-SOLVING

You and your team are poking around the edges but not directly getting a grip on the real issue. First seek clarity. Rinse away the debris in your thought process *(Mint 28)*. Leverage your YQ, your Yield Question *(Mint 7)* with your awesome brain power *(Mint 24)*. Probe simply (*Mint 3*). Write down your thoughts *(Mint 90)*. And beware of grabbing what is instead of grasping what could be (*Mint 25*).

SPEAKING

You and/or your staff have to make a presentation to the rest of the company. Already the butterflies are swirling around your collective heads. Calm down, then: Wake up your audience as if you were kissing Sleeping Beauty or Prince Charming   *(Mint 100)*. Then FLIRT with your audience (*Mint 71*). Leverage your face value

(Mint 72) in particular and your body language in general *(Mint 73)*. Tune in to your audience's needs and interests *(Mint 76)* with the proper tone *(Mint 99)* and pacing *(Mint 83)*. Make LOVE—Look On Vitally Engaged —with your audience *(Mint 70)*. Write a Pre-Script-ion for your audience that will give you more control over the dosage (intensity of the message) and duration of your speech *(Mint 88.)* Rehearse *(Mint 98)* and practice your public speaking skills regularly at your own pace at a Toastmasters Meeting *(Mint 101)*.

THINKING

You and your team are always on the run. Slow down. Take time to meditate *(Mint 2)*. Simmer your thoughts as if they were stirring in a crock pot *(Mint 74)*. Recruit a sounding board to echo your thoughts *(Mint 1)*. Open your mind with more funnel vision than tunnel vision *(Mint 23)*. Hone the possibilities with the power of the paradox   *(Mint 84)*.

TEAMWORK

You and your staff need to work even better together as a team. Take the time to sense and support the feelings of others *(Mint 37).)* Celebrate your "Navel Intelligence" connection to others *(Mint 39)*. Declare your interdependence *(Mint 44)*. Balance the needs of all without infringing on the needs of one *(Mint 56)*. Support each other *(Mint 47)*. Interact with others *(Mint 59)*. Celebrate diversity *(Mint 9)*. And dedicate a team room *(Mint 97)*.

CREATIVITY
Part I

*"There is incremental improvement
to anything.
The only reason we stop creating
is that we run out of time or budget."*

-David Kelley, Founder, IDEO

Mint 1

Listening to Yourself THINK!

Reading time 3:36

Wandering aimlessly into his backyard late at night, Tim-the-Tool-Man is troubled again. The star of the 1990s television sitcom *Home Improvement* needs help thinking through a problem. And somehow, Wilson — his next door neighbor — is always within ear-shot to help Tim the Tool Man find his way again. Wilson's face is always partially hidden by a fence or a camera angle – a theatrical technique that lends even more credence to his auditory role as Tim's sounding board. Every leader needs his or her Wilson. Every leader needs a sounding board – someone to bounce ideas off, someone to echo your thoughts so you hear them more clearly, someone you trust to help you validate or rectify your reality. How do find that Someone? How do you develop your own Wilson, your own sounding board? Try booking ONE friend at a time rather than seeking to Facebook a lot of friends all the time.

Booking that ONE friend is vital—the kind of friend developed through heart-felt listening to and learning from each other, the kind of friend that comes to discern parts of your personality that you don't see in yourself. For example, a friend and confidant like Wilson discerned that the letters in Tim-the-Tool-Man's given name (Tim Taylor) is an anagram for "Morality (or more precisely moralitty)." Who knew? Wilson knew. That sense of discovery, identity and intimacy develops only over time and with patience. Leaders know only too well there is no app to help you focus more on meeting face-to-face, thinking head-to-head, working together shoulder to shoulder, or seeing eye-to-eye. The most effective leaders know their lives are more effectively connected NOT on-line but IN LINE —in person—

with others at your grocery store, deli, coffee house etc. There IN LINE –face-to-face– you don't need a mouse or keyboard to click with a friend. All you need is a smile and a common interest stirred with an openness to learn from, to share with, and to listen to. Yet the flurry of bits and bytes invading 24/7 from cyberspace keep gnawing away at the potential of a leader. In a guest lecture to plebes at West Point Academy, a former Yale University leadership development professor challenged the 19-year-old freshmen to invest themselves personally in more face-to-face, no-screen required relationships. "Instead of having one or two true friends that we can sit and talk to for three hours at a time, we have 968 'friends' that we never actually talk to," William Deresiewicz said. "Instead we just bounce one-line messages off them a hundred times a day. This is not friendship. This is distraction."

Yet, too many leaders say they are too busy to seek the solitude that Deresiewicz says is "the essence of leadership." But how many would-be leaders are just too busy being busy; too busy paying homage to the Texting and Tweeting gods, and too busy to be a friend to SomeONE let alone find a friend with anyone? How do you wrestle the hands of time long enough away from your time-consuming technology as you thumb your way merrily along the cyber highway? How do you take the time to make a friend and dedicate the time to be a friend? First make a friend of yourself. Get comfortable in your own skin. And bounce your thinking off a sounding board.

Today's ImproveMINT

*Establish a Sounding Board for your thoughts
to keep your leadership thinking in mint condition.*

●

Making Yourself At "OM"

Reading time 3:46

Om is the centuries-old meditation mantra where the incantation of the voice hums the body's muscles into a state of relaxation. Ommmmmmm channels the mind to focus on the important no matter how demanding the urgent. Ommmmmmm turns solitude into a catalyst for breakthrough ideas. Thomas Edison felt at "om." The inventor of the light bulb and inventor of nearly 1200 patents nurtured his own solitude day in and day out. He disciplined himself to sit in silence for an hour a day THINKING. Likewise billionaire J. Paul Getty disciplined himself to sit alone in his study for an hour or two each day THINKING. And Mohandas Gandhi took off one day each week to "listen to my inner voice," to listen to his THINKING. The most effective leaders schedule a daily meeting with themselves – to think. Historians tell us that Jesus scheduled a meeting with himself in the desert; Mohammed scheduled a meeting with himself in the mountains, and Saint Benedict scheduled a meeting with himself in a cave.

It takes a strong dose of discipline to develop this kind of affinity for listening to yourself and ultimately tuning in to the most appropriate sounding board. After all it is not easy for human beings with a bias for action (a.k.a. a leader) to sit still for an extended time period. Pioneers in the wagon train days would even bang their pots and pans in the stillness of the dark when it got too quiet. Then the wolves could be heard from miles away making the pioneers even more uncomfortable in the eerie silence. Then in the desolate darkness of the wilderness in the wild West the pioneers also had to fight off even more voracious and nefarious wolves of self-doubt and fear. These wolves of the mind gnawed at the hearts and souls of the pioneers. These wolves of the mind howled in the isolated blackness and blankness of the night.

These wolves of the mind slashed and scratched at the hopes of the pioneers with a frightening, debilitating vengeance that philosopher Blaise Pascal called a devastating "nothingness" where the quiet is so very disquieting. The most effective leaders overcome their deafening sounds of silence –their fears of nothingness and their illusions of emptiness. Maybe that's why leaders around the world have a Meditation Room in the United Nations building where they can confront the demons in their minds and where leaders can turn Pascal's "nothingness" into SOMETHINGNESS — no matter how eerie the silence, no matter how isolated the executive suite or how loud the wolves howl.

Find your muse, your Yoda, your Wilson to help you make sense of the solitude just like Tom Hanks did in the movie Cast Away. Hanks' character is marooned on an island. He's alone but not lonely. He's lost but not abandoned. He someone to bounce his thoughts off of, something to help him overcome his fear of nothingness, someone to help him find more purpose and meaning in his situation in the middle of nowhere. Oh, that someone may look like just a volleyball, but to him it's his friend, his confidant, his answer to the banging the pots and pans to ward off those howling wolves of the night. To Tom Hanks' cast away character, Wilson is the name of a person not just a brand stamped on a volleyball -- a person who is helping him leverage his solitude and feel more at "OM."

Today's ImproveMINT

Leverage solitude to keep
your leadership thinking in mint condition

●

Make It Simple Not Simpler

Reading time: 3:05

Gracefully waving his arms, the minister announced that his sermon on this Sunday morning would be "childishly, simple." He paused and then added very seriously: "I really worked at it to make it that simple." Leaders work very hard to make complex ideas THAT simple. They maintain the richness of the context without discounting the content. These simple-minding leaders are anything but simple-minded. They enrich themselves and others with the same train of thought that billionaire Warren Buffett tracks in leading investment strategy. "Successful investing is simple but not easy," Buffett says.

So too, is successful leading: It's simple but not easy. In fact it takes great courage and a confident sense of the value in vulnerability to be simple, according to Jack Welch, the former chairman of the General Electric Company. "You can't believe how hard it is for people to be simple, how much they fear being simple," Welch says. "They worry that if they're simple, people will think they're simple-minded. In reality, of course, it's just the reverse. Clear tough-minded people are the most simple." Yet insecure managers hide behind complexity. They snow you with a blizzard of paperwork. They drown you with a deluge of information. Maintaining a complicated life "is a great way to avoid changing," observed Elaine St. James, author of *Simplify Your Life*: "We become comfortable with our problems." It's a movie that Welch has seen too many times. Call it the Complex Cinema where "frightened nervous managers use thick, convoluted planning books and busy slides filled with everything they've known since childhood." Real leaders don't hide behind anything. They strive to bare all. They strive for transparency. They know "to be simple is to be great," as author Ralph Waldo Emerson noted.

That's why real leaders seek to make things simple – and not simpler as Albert Einstein so famously noted. How? With leadership rooted in clarity. Unencumbered. Uncluttered. Unfettered. And judgment that draws meaningful distinctions and enterprising connections.

- Real leaders don't eliminate. They illuminate.
- Real leaders don't subtract. They extract.
- Real leaders don't confine. They refine.

Sure, you can always make something simpler by denuding it, by stripping parts from it, by throwing the baby out with the bath water.

But denuding would be deluding.

Real leaders portion and package information strategically rather than routinely slice and dice it, trim it or grind it. Real leaders embrace the notion of scientist Martin Fischer who observed: "Knowledge is a process of piling up facts. Wisdom lies in their simplification." That's why real leaders simplify to amplify and that's why being simply minded is the secret sauce in every leader's problem-solving kettle. Even childishly simple—if they work at it.

Today's ImproveMINT

Simplify to keep
your leadership thinking in mint condition

●

Mint 4

Yabba Dabba Dooooo On Monday Morning Too

Reading time: 3:38

Yabba Dabba Dooooooo! The 5 o'clock whistle just blew and Fred Flintstone unleashes his signature response: "Yabba Dabba Dooooooo!" The work week is through. Millions of dissatisfied workers know the malaise that so many research studies confirm among workers in America. Too many employees show up for work and mentally checkout long before the end of the day. They may be physically present but are soulfully absent. They struggle so much WORKING for a living that they forget how to work AT living. They may not appreciate the difference between them being at WORK and their BEING at work. For too many of those workers, having a fulfilling work experience is something that can only happen at lunch time. So how do you insure that you bring your "A" game to work every day? How do you help yourself or your employees stay in the game wide awake as long as it takes? You lead them and yourself. ON PURPOSE.

With a purpose well defined, you can help others revitalize their job as something that energizes more than exhausts, something that invigorates more than denigrates, something that turns the ordinary into the extraordinary, and something that turns the frustration of a job into the inspiration of a Job. Mr. or Mrs. Yabba Dabba Dooooooooo might feel a bit more exhilarated than exhausted on the job if he or she understood --more fully-- the PURPOSE of his or her repetitive and routine work. In Fred Flintstone's case, he is digging more than rocks out of a quarry. He is creating the building blocks for what could become a grand office building or a new arena. Or even a cathedral. The key is to consistently update yourself and/or the Fred Flintstones on your staff of the critical importance of —and need for — THEIR work. Help them understand specifically how their individual puzzle piece of the business fits into the big picture. Show them —and remind yourself— how that big picture would be missing something crucial if they weren't there to do their jobs, no matter how routine, no matter how seemingly insignificant. Give your individual staff people their Come-to-Clarence Moment long before their obligatory annual review. You recall Clarence, the guardian angel in the movie *It's a Wonderful Life.* The angel reminds us of the dignity and worth of each individual, their impact on the growth and well-being of others, and the cascading and devastating changes that would ensue in lives all around them if they had not been born. As Clarence says: "A person touches so many other lives that when he isn't around he leaves an awful hole, doesn't he?

Leaders plug that hole when they are plugged-IN to the lives of others — living and working more ON PURPOSE, living and working on something bigger than themselves, something that "optimizes the human condition" as author Michael Novak observes in his book *Business as a Calling*. Inspired employees working ON PURPOSE pay themselves – in self-respect, self-confidence and self-worth. Every day is Pay Day. Working on Purpose, they become engaged in their work long before they are at work. They see the intended cathedrals in their minds. And their Get-er-Done energy, spirit and drive all but mutes that 5 o'clock whistle in a symphony of creativity and productivity, a symphony that you may even hear on Monday morning when still another engaging, interesting, and challenging work week begins. On purpose. Yabba Dabba Dooooooo!

Today's ImproveMINT
Emphasize the purpose of work
to keep your leadership thinking in mint condition.

●

Mint 5

Stories Breathe Life Into the Bottom Line

Reading time: 3:18

Storytime seemed so real. So thrilling. The professional children's storyteller had just finished a 30-minute performance at a pre-school. A 4-year-old boy excitedly ran up to the storyteller, yanked on her hand and smiled: "Hey, thanks for the movies!" The vivid story captured his imagination. The words painted a picture in his mind. The storyteller's engaging tone and exciting inflection tuned her voice into what seemed the surround sound quality of a theater. Only the popcorn seemed to be missing from the boy's "movie"— and moving —experience.

No wonder storytelling is a key leadership skill, according to Harvard professor Howard Gardner. In his book *Leading Minds,* Gardner observes that "leaders achieve their effectiveness chiefly through the stories they relate, through their ability to hold the attention of others." Capturing attention and garnering the hearts and minds of listeners, stories are more convincing than facts, according to research conducted at Stanford University. Why?

1. Stories get to the heart of the issue first and foremost, according to Noel Tichy, the author of *The Leadership Engine* and a professor at the University of Michigan. Stories "engage listeners on an emotional and intuitive level that is rarely touched by the purely rational argument," Tichy notes.

2. Stories in fact sell more than simply tell. Stories humanize, energize and mobilize. The most effective leaders know that each story is like

another log on the fire brightening, warming and comforting those huddled around.

3. Anthropologist Margaret Mead called story-telling a "perpetuated experience" that truly distinguishes human groups.

4. Stories can be more of an antidote than simply an anecdote. Stories can clear up a toxic situation and mobilize the necessary change in behavior.

With that kind of influence, storytellers have always been held in high esteem. In fact, during the Renaissance storytellers attained greater status than Lords, the property owners. Their stories gave us "better insights into the depths of past centuries than grave and voluminous chronicles," observed author Ralph Waldo Emerson. With stories, leaders unveil the nuance of an organization, its particularities and its particulars. With stories, leaders pump blood into the corporate body-- blood that feeds the bottom line, blood that infuses employees, stockholders, customers and other stakeholders with a greater sense of loyalty, of belonging and of making a difference. And with stories leaders cement a more powerful emotional bond beyond the overwhelming visual flood of You Tube, internet streaming and gaming in all their digital dynamism. What? More vivid that screen sensations? More vivid than video games? No way you say. Well now hold on there VIDEO BREATH and listen to a television industry icon producer. "It's your ear more than your eye that keeps you at your television set," said Don Hewitt, the creator and producer for more than 30 years of CBS-Television's 60 Minutes. "It's what you hear more than what you see that holds your interest." Just ask that 4-year old boy who saw a page-turner of a movie without ever seeing a screen.

Today's ImproveMINT

Share your personal stories
to keep your leadership thinking in mint condition.

●

Parachuting:
From Fright to Insight

Reading time: 3:07

Precariously perched, he stood just inches away from the plane's open door, just inches away from the engine's deafening roar, just inches away from the wind's screaming call. And just inches away from his first parachute jump. He looked down. His eyes blurred. His palms moistened. Fright drained the saliva from his mouth. Sweat trickled down his forehead. Wind flooded his face. Wrestling against that 80-mile-an-hour wind, he struggled to fling his legs out the side of the single engine airplane. He planted his toe on the 3-inch wide step. And let go. Plunging, plummeting, toppling and tumbling, he fell 242 feet in four seconds on a static line that opened the parachute automatically.

Suddenly, the screaming air quieted.

The roaring engine faded. His fearful, tearful eyes opened in awe wonder and majesty. He looked up and there it was: the most beautiful flower he ever saw blossoming in the sky. His red canopy opened like a 32-foot wide tulip petal blossoming atop the 20-foot tall stem of harness rope. It was so peaceful, so placid, so pacific, so soothing, so serene, and so silent. So hushed. He felt that he could almost whisper in God's ear.

As he dangled from that 40-pound pack of cloth — like a puppet on string -- he looked down some 3,000 feet below. The utility poles looked like toothpicks. The river looked like a thick black ribbon. The field looked like a huge patchwork quilt. He pulled the turn toggles and made like a human top spinning around to enjoy the panorama. He had the world literally at his feet. Suddenly, the ground below started rushing up. Suddenly, the utility poles looked like redwood trees. Suddenly, the river looked like a huge table cloth. Suddenly, the horizon began to explode out of the ground. And then suddenly, SLAM! He hit the ground with a sobering thud.

- Stunned. He sat in the middle of a cornfield and wondered if he was dead.
- Stunned. He lunged for his 10-inch high boots and wondered if those boots were still attached to his feet. He wondered if his feet were still attached to him.

Relieved. A smile washed across his face. From fear to cheer. From 4,000 feet to his own two feet. From fright to insight. He didn't die. He was born. Born with exhilaration for life, a life more invigorating, a life that gets a jump on fear. His first parachute jump taught him this important leadership lesson:

Look at problem solving from all directions – in particular — opposite the direction you are focusing.

Consider his parachuting plight: perched at the plane's open door and looking down 4,000 feet, he was scared. Then just four seconds later looking up at the canopy on his parachute, he was so exhilarated, so thrilled. Indeed, where you stand on an issue depends on where you sit. (See page 49, Mint 16.)

Today's ImproveMINT

Parlay your sense of perspective
to keep your leadership thinking in mint condition.

Mint 7

What's Your YQ?
Reading time: 3:11

Questions can be insightful, thoughtful, and probing. Good leaders answer questions. Better leaders question answers. And the best leaders question questions. In fact, the best leaders are always striving to raise their YQ —their Yield Questions— to gain more meaning than mere answers. Like the farmer who seeks a greater crop yield per acre, so too the leader leverages his or her YQ to yield more meaningful ideas per thought— ideas that spark discovery; insights that spur innovation and initiatives that spearhead achievement. Questions probe new paths of self-discovery. When you question yourself, you think. When you question input, you judge. When you question output, you evaluate. When you question both input and output, systemically and systematically, you improve.

Consider the YQ—the Yield Question—that Benjamin Zander asks himself as the conductor of the Boston Philharmonic Orchestra. He defines success as his ability to bring out the best performance in each of his musicians. He measures his success by "how many shining eyes I have around me." If he doesn't see that shining in the eyes of his musicians, he poses this insightful and leadership leveraging Yield Question: "Who am I being right now that my musicians eyes are not beaming?" Then the leader in him adapts and adjust to enhance both his and the orchestra's performance. Indeed Yield Questions focus your performance and enhance leadership as Max De Pree, former CEO and author, writes in his book *Leadership Jazz*: "The quality of our work as leaders and the quality of our lives depends significantly on the questions we ask and the people about whom we ask the questions." In his book, *Why Leaders Can't Lead*, Warren Bennis writes that truth begins with questions. Yield Questions enhance teamwork.

in his book *Out of the Crisis,* W. Edwards Deming writes that teamwork requires everyone to "sharpen each other's wits with questions." And Dan Goleman in his book, *The Creative Spirit* writes that "Asking the right question is crucial for creative insight." For example, instead of issuing a statement *(Do it this way.)* to correct an employee's performance behavior, ask Yield Question: *"Can I show you another way that may help?"* In general, questions can either cap or tap enormous potential, depending on the flexibility of the questioner to make a connection to something new rather than pay attention to something he or she already knew. Armed with questions, leaders seek new opportunities in the same way an explorer seeks new frontiers. In fact, the verb "To question" stems from the Latin word (*quaerer*) which means "to seek." Leaders, like scientists, seek to unlock the unknown with questions. As Dr. Werner Heisenberg, the father of quantum physics, observed: "Nature does not reveal its secrets. It only responds to a method of questioning." So does leadership.

- With your Yield Question —your YQ — you will be able to mobilize ideas, issues and concerns with impact, insight and intensity so that they are heard, understood and acted upon with courage, conviction and confidence.
- With your Yield Question— your YQ—you will light a flame of creativity, a flame that ignites the artist in you; a flame that sparks the poet in you and a flame that flares the philosopher in you.
- With your Yield Question— your YQ—you will embrace a can-do, will-do spirit, energy and drive to capitalize on change. With your Yield Question — your YQ —you will lead. Without question.

Today's ImproveMINT

Increase your YQ –your Yield Questions –
to keep your leadership thinking in mint condition.

●

Mint 8

Are You Forty or Forte?

Reading time: 3:43

D reading your 40th birthday? I did. But I survived and even thrived because I practiced one of the most critical leadership skills: framing the problem or issue so you can better cope with it, learn from it and grow because of it. What if you saw yourself at 40 stepping onto a launching pad rather than onto a guillotine? A launching pad? How absurd!

Tell that to Jules Verne, the visionary author who saw deep into the heavens (*From the Earth to the Moon*), deep into the sea *(Twenty Thousand Leagues Under the Sea)*, deep into the center of the earth *(Journey Into The Center of the Earth)* and deep into the center of me.

At least it seemed that way.

Jules Verne helped me see the 40-year-old version of me in a refreshingly new and different way. On page 117 in his book *From the Earth to the Moon*, Jules Verne describes the first manned moon launching 104 years before Neil Armstrong. Significantly, Jules Verne launches his man to the moon (actually three men) with a count UP 37...38...39..... You guessed it. At the count of 40, the rocket ignites, propelling the three fictional astronauts to go higher, faster and farther than any other human has gone before. What if turning 40 could be my lift off, launching me into a higher self-orbit than ever before in my previous 14,610 days on earth? Now after 350,640 hours of refueling and recharging my batteries, I was in for the blast of my life. After all, Julius Caesar didn't take command of his first army until age 41. Abraham Lincoln, Henry Ford and Albert

Einstein achieved their greatest success after they turned
40.

- At 40 Jonas Salk developed a polio vaccine.
- At 40, John Glenn became the first American to orbit
  the earth.
- At 40, Florence Nightingale founded a nursing school.
- At 40, newly married poet Elizabeth Barrett Browning
  wrote her famous poem: *How Do I Love Thee?*
- And at 40, Hank Aaron broke Babe Ruth's career home
  run hitting record.

At 40, I sensed more fusion than confusion in my life.
There was a sense of parts coming together to form a
stronger whole. I couldn't claim, as Confucius did on his
40th birthday, that I knew all I was then. But in turning 40, I
was gaining more stability much like a sword's forte — the
strongest part of the blade. I thought of myself evolving,
getting stronger, becoming forte more than forty. Life at 40
now made more sense to me than ever before. I even found
more meaning in the music I grew up with in general and
The Beatles in particular--especially in realizing that *The
Beatles* first appeared live on American television on the
40th day of the year (February 9, 1964, *The Ed Sullivan
Show*). Of course my body still aches at times. Reading
between the lines these days takes on a scarier meaning
every morning when I look into the mirror. My actions creak
louder than my words. "Outta Sight" – a favorite expression
in my college days—smacks of a grim reality. And I can see
myself in that *Peanuts* comic strip where Charlie Brown says
he's worried about his 40-year-old father who sits at the
kitchen table eating cold cereal and looking wistfully at
pictures in his high school yearbook. But so what if the
digital recorder wound into my mind is no longer on fast-
forward. I've found the PLAY button. Forte!

Today's ImproveMINT

*Reframe an issue to better solve it and
keep your leadership thinking in mint condition.*

●

Uncorking Bottled-Up Creativity

Reading time: 2:57

Wine glasses, sparkling and empty, looked conspicuously out of place in this corporate business environment—a team project room--especially first thing on Monday morning. The team leader was pouring what seemed to be white wine from an elegantly stemmed bottle as her team members assembled for their regular update meeting. "Yes, I know it's still early but I think a toast is in order," the team leader said. She served the filled wine glasses to her seven team members who all looked at her like she just had lost it. After all, alcohol in a project room or anywhere on campus was against company policy. And besides the work day had just started. Most folks were still on their second cup of coffee.

The team leader smiled and said, "No, no. This only looks like wine. It's just water." Now everyone thought she had snapped. She took a sip. And then she offered her toast. "I've always been intrigued that you can make white wine from red grapes." She explained that white Zinfandel wine is created from the same grape as red Zinfandel. "Likewise, you made white wine out of red grapes," the team leader said. "You used old resources in new ways in bringing this project this far on time and under budget. So I toast your resourcefulness." The team leader sipped her cold refreshing "bottled" water with a touch of lemon that she had poured earlier into an empty wine bottle she brought from home to stage her demonstration. Her team members hesitantly first smelled the liquid in their wine glasses and then drank to the toast. They were relieved and then delighted to realize they were drinking good old H_2O. Their team leader hadn't lost it. Yet. In fact their team leader gained plenty of credibility and memorability in reinforcing her message to her team: using limited resources in a variety of creative ways is a key to a project's success and to the organization's ultimate growth. As authors George Land and Beth Jarman write in their book in *Breakpoint and Beyond*: "The growth potential of any system is fulfilled by connecting with the different and the dissimilar rather than building on similarities."

Indeed, connecting The Different makes a significant difference. The team leader could have simply just stated that fact at the team meeting that she wanted her team to focus on greater diversity in how resources are used. But as a leader she also wanted to make a more lasting impression much like the time she passed around a pink flamingo stuffed toy. Her point? Know the source of your resource. Flamingos are naturally gray. They get their pink color from the algae they eat. Another time, the team leader passed around a photo book on the Lipizzan horses, the stunningly elegant white horses of Spanish royalty fame. Her point? Stay vigilant. Realize that what you see is not what you get all time. A resource can change significantly over time. Those wonderously white horses are born black. "It takes a creative mindset to see what the eye can't immediately see and mine the most out of our resources," the team leader said. She lift her "wine" glass and beamed enthusiastically: "Next time we'll be toasting champagne at a fancy restaurant celebrating our new product launch." Chances are then the team leader will find it hard to resist another salute to diversity. She knows of course that champagne (white in color) is made with more red grapes (Pinot noir and Pinot Meunier) than white grapes (chardonnay). Cheers!

Today's ImproveMINT

Diversify your resources to keep
your leadership thinking in mint condition.

●

Coloring Beyond The Bottom Line

Reading time: 3:14

B utcher paper covering the exquisitely polished table in the executive conference room seemed out of place as the 11 vice presidents filed into the palatial mahogany and marble suite for a strategy session. The president called the meeting to order and immediately surprised everyone. He passed out supersized purple crayons. Then, the president sat back, stroked his crayon as if it were a fine cigar. Then he cradled that cigar as if it were a treasure to behold and said: "There's power in this crayon, power that we can use to draw greater profitability and productively, power to create our own business climate no matter how lousy the economy."

The executives smirked at the sophomoric theatrics. Their body language clearly told the president just how ridiculous and irrelevant he sounded. No matter. The president ignored the tension in the room. Instead, he began talking about his childhood. He remembered his mother reading a book to him more than 40 years ago about a guy named Harold who would take his purple crayon and creatively draw himself a hot air balloon when he fell off a cliff. He said the lessons in that book— Crockett Johnson's *Harold and the Purple Crayon*— sparked a sense of initiative, imagination and ingenuity that helped him create a profitable company over the last six years as president. But in the last six months, a worldwide economic downturn was taking its toll on the company's bottom line. Business prospects looked as bleak as that blank sheet of paper sprawled over the conference room table. Gripping his purple crayon with conviction, the president began coloring on that large sheet of butcher paper. He invited others to join him in "creating our own air balloon to heighten our profitability." Sure the economy was scaring even the most seasoned executives, he allowed. The president confessed at times he even felt the fright Harold must have felt in that book when he came face to face with a scary dragon.

"Harold was so frightened that his hand shook," the president demonstrated. His crayon skidded over the butcher paper with a shaky hand that left a jagged purple line, much like the waves of an ocean. "But Harold simply took that purple crayon – the same purple crayon that you are holding right now. He looked at those jagged lines like so many waves crushing in on him, jagged lines that look much like our profitability chart right now — plenty of ups and downs, mostly downs—and Harold quickly drew a boat and put a sail on it."

Then the president, resolute and resilient, got up from the table and said: "Let's get busy building our sailboat this morning. We have all the tools we need in our hands, in ourselves."

The smirks on the face of the executives turned to grins. They got it. The purple crayon metaphor reminded the president just how resourceful his company and its executives were. Together they could draw their own hot air balloon, no matter how steep the cliff they're on right now. Parlay your purple crayon and make your mark. Resourcefully.

Today's ImproveMINT

Rekindle your innovative spirit
with children's books
to keep your leadership thinking
in mint condition.

Mint 11

Raising the Flag
In your ImagiNATION

Reading time: 3:42

Have you ever felt like running away from it all? Of course you have. Oh, the freedom, the sense of wonder and opportunity over that next horizon! Let's go. Let's run away today just like that   11-year-old boy did so many years ago. He stowed away on a ship bound for India. But then his dad caught up with him just before the ship headed out to the open sea. The boy was punished. His mom scolded him: "If you ever run away again, travel only in your imagination." Jules Verne listened. The same Jules Verne who would travel in his imagination as a famous science fiction author. The same Jules Verne who navigated *20,000 Leagues Under the Sea*. The same Jules Verne who embarked on a *Journey to the Center of the Earth.* And the same Jules Verne who launched a manned vehicle to the moon —*From Earth to Moon*—104 years before Neil Armstrong first took one small step for man, one giant leap for mankind. Ah, the power — the POWER—of your imagination. So powerful that Napoleon said imagination rules the world. So powerful that Albert Einstein said: "Imagination is more important than knowledge." And so powerful that poet William Blake said that with your imagination you could: *"See a world in a grain of sand and a heaven in a wild flower. Hold infinity in the palm of your hand and eternity in an hour."*

How do you fire up your imagination like that? Forget the rose-colored glasses. Get away from the familiar. Don a pair of walking shoes, hiking boots, tennis shoes, golf shoes etc. Get out of your office/workplace. And run away to another nation — your ImagiNATION. Remember the scene in the movie *Miracle on 34th Street* when Kris Kringle is trying to define the Christmas spirit in general and Santa Claus in particular to a very skeptical five-year-old girl? He says: "Now you've heard of the French nation, the British nation, well this is the ImagiNATION. It's a wonderful place." And how do you get to this place called the ImagiNATION? You already have your passport –your curiosity. Follow it. Change your venue. Change your routine. Be abnormal for an hour or so each day. Do something different. Instead of taking your dog for a walk, let your dog take you for a walk. Instead of running your usual two-mile route in the morning, try running half as far— twice as much (out and back) —and give yourself two viewpoints on the road to your ImagiNATION. No matter how you raise the flag on your ImagiNATION, chances are you'll always come back to your work more rejuvenated, more refreshed, and more productive. Then with your imagination flaring you may even feel like you're wielding more power than any warrior every dreamed. At least that's how they saluted the ImagiNATION of Thomas Edison during the dedication ceremony of his museum in Menlo Park, NJ. They said the inventor of the light bulb and 1200 other patents:

> *"...led no armies into battle, conquered no countries, enslaved no peoples, yet he wields a power the magnitude of which no warrior ever dreamed."*

Leaders wield that kind of power in a land that has no borders—their ImagiNATION. Run away today into your ImagiNATION.

Today's ImproveMINT

Use your passport
into your ImagiNATION
to keep your leadership thinking
in mint condition.

●

Mint 12

5 Ways To Ride
The RODEO of Creativity

Reading time: 6:04

Rodeo! Let's rodeo! Bronco-busting. Bull-riding. Calf-roping. You can't even imagine how wild it must be to compete in the most dangerous eight seconds in sports where a 2,000 pound bull can throw you around like a ragdoll.

No doubt, rodeo performers have to be more flexible, more versatile, more creative to stay alive and thrive on that ton of emotion in motion on four legs. So let's use the word **RODEO** as an acrostic for five ways you can become a more creative leader:

Random Selection

Randomly select two words out of the dictionary. Then look for a creative connection between them. Take for example the words: rock and pet. The creative connection is a simile: how is a pet like a rock? How is a rock like a pet? And more significantly how is a rock not like a pet and a pet not like a rock? That was the creative connection that inventor Gary Dahl developed to counter the complaints of his friends about the care and feeding of their real pets.

That kind of random connection between a rock and pet sparked the interest of 1.3 million people to pay $4 each for a rock. But there was nothing random about the sales pitch that included a 32-page owner's manual in how to take care and train your Pet Rock which of course never needs to be walked or scooped up from behind. You can use the same random approach to create other similes that broaden the scope of a subject. Take for example the word "life." Now randomly select a word from the dictionary. Then connect those two words or concepts with the bridge phrase "is like."

So if you selected the word "confetti," you would then look for a creative connection between the two words: How is life like confetti? Or how is confetti not like life?

Orienting

You can also be creative by orienting two different things more directly with each other rather than randomly like this:

1. Historians tell us that Johann Gutenberg's press in 1439 oriented two previously unconnected ideas: the wine press and the coin punch. Gutenberg put the coin punch under the force of a wine press so that it left images on paper.

2. Physicians at London's Great Osmond Street Hospital oriented two previously unconnected ideas and devised a more efficient surgical handoff between surgery and intensive care when they studied the precision of a Formula One pit crew.

3. A Notre Dame football coach oriented two previously unconnected ideas and invented a new offensive formation when Knute Rockne associated a burlesque chorus dancing routine with four running backs that gave rise to the famed Four Horsemen of Notre Dame.

4. The first self-service grocery store in 1916 oriented two previously unconnected ideas: the self-service system of a cafeteria and a grocery. In four years, Clarence Saunders oriented himself from a $20 a week clerk to a $4 million grocery empire.

Distorting

1. The first ice cream cone was invented when a waffle was distorted at the St. Louis World's Fair in 1903. The waffle was rolled into the first ice cream cone when the nearby ice cream vendor ran out of cups.

2. Napoleon distorted the traditional rules of warfare in capturing an Austrian army. The beaten Austrian general complained that Napoleon "doesn't know anything about the rules of war. First he attacks us from the rear, and then he comes to our left. It's preposterous. He goes against every tradition."

Exchanging

1. Ice cream lovers rejoice! The first sundae was invented when chocolate syrup was exchanged for the soda in a cup of ice cream. The exchange circumvented a law forbidding ice cream sodas to be sold on Sundays in Evanston, IL.

2. An entrepreneur purchased his boyhood home. He wanted to restore the brick house to its original state. But the most recent owners of the home had painted the red- brick siding white and nothing seemed to take the white paint off the bricks without discoloring the bricks from their original color. He creatively solved the problem with an exchange of the bricks, turning them inside out. The inside red-colored bricks now became the outside of the house.

3. A Polish artist Josef Szajna was confined to a standing cell 3 feet by 3 feet during World War II. From that tiny spot, he could see a tiny blue patch of sky in the little window overhead. In in his mind's eye, he exchanged that spot of blue as if it were his own blue canvass. And he painted to his heart's delight and survived.

Overstating

1. George Crum, a chef in the 1850s, overstated the thinness of the potatoes he was frying and invented potato chips. He was trying to satisfy the complaints of a guest at Moon's Lake House in Saratoga Springs, NY. The guest complained that his fried potatoes were not thin enough. He sent the potatoes back to the kitchen three times. Finally the head chef got mad. George Crum angrily sliced the potatoes paper thin, fried them, and sarcastically served them to the guest. The guest was delighted and so are millions of other potato chip lovers today.

2. Another example of overstating gave birth to the first Neighborhood Crime Watch programs. Edward deBono, the author of numerous books on creative thinking, posed this over-statement: what if a policeman had six eyes? That over-statement sparked the creative thinking that led to the formation of the Neighborhood Crime Watch program.

So let's **RODEO** in your creative leading. Utilize those five strategies—Random Selection & Connection, Orienting, Distorting, Exchanging, and Overstating—in sparking your effective leadership. Bulldoze your way through problems creatively with your own RODEO.

Today's ImproveMINT

Ride the RODEO of creativity
to keep your leadership thinking in mint condition.

●

Slipping into a Girdle of Innovation

Reading time: 3:28

Wearing a gas mask, the vice president walked into her staff meeting late as usual. Eyes widened and jaws dropped around the table. Her staff couldn't make sense of what they were seeing. "No, I'm not a terrorist and I am not going to blow the place up," she laughed while taking the gas mask off her face. You could almost hear the collective sigh of relief among the staff, their hearts still pounding faster than normal, their breathing still accelerated from the visual shock. "But maybe this gas mask can spark our creative discussion this morning on new product ideas," the vice president added in ramping up her teaching point.

She explained that Kleenex, the $1.2 billion facial tissue and category leader, initially was developed as a filter for a gas mask during World War I, then as a facial cream remover in 1924 and finally as a facial tissue that today catches runny noses in 140 countries! In each new product launch, the creative thinkers responded to a changing customer need, she observed. The vice president picked up the gas mask in one hand and a box of Kleenex in the other and quoted Aristotle: "Everything is both what is and what it may become."

Resourceful leaders use old things in new ways. Even girdles: Yes girdles. Turns out that girdles —back in the day—were made from a polyurethane material that has the same elasticity of the heart. Doctors used the girdle to construct the first artificial heart valve. Call it wiggle room of another kind, the kind of wiggle room that innovative leaders bring to creative problem-solving. That girdle story illustrates that leaders use whatever resources are available in new and different ways. Even women's skirts: In the Civil War, Confederate troops wanted to construct an observation balloon. They needed 980 yards of silk material. Women in Savannah, GA donated their silk skirts to make the observation balloon.

Indeed innovative leaders use whatever resources are available in new and different ways. Even diapers: Fire fighters noticed that everything in a dump burned except the diapers. They found out what chemicals comprised the diapers and used that chemical in a special spray as a fire-retardant to save homes from a wildfire in Florida.

- Be resourceful and you could use the twisted sinew of a moose or a deer or the skin of a snapping turtle to become the bow as the innovative Chippewa Indians did.
- Be resourceful and you could become like artist Benjamin West who used the hairs of a cat to make his own paint brushes.
- Be resourceful and you could become like inventor Thomas Edison. He found a thread in his wife's sewing basket that became a filament for the world's first long-lasting light bulb.
- Be resourceful and you could take insulation for copper wire and turn it into a non-stick cooking pan (Teflon).

The leadership lesson is clear: leverage your wiggle room of innovation and become a resourceful leader.

Today's ImproveMINT

Creatively use your existing resources
to keep your leadership thinking in mint condition

●

Squeezing Innovation Out of a Teddy Bear

Reading time: 3:58

When you innovate, you find a new use for something old and familiar. That's what leaders do. They make old things new again. Innovative leaders turned a stuffed teddy bear into a life -saving tool for heart patients. Meet Sir Cough-a-Lot, a teddy bear who comes to the rescue of patients recovering from open-heart surgery. Here's how resourceful Sir Cough-a-Lot is:

Put your hands lightly on your stomach and cough. You feel the muscles in your stomach contract and pull when you cough. Now imagine your stomach as if it were a blanket full of stitches. Just think of the pain you would suffer when you have to force yourself to cough up the festering poison in your stomach called phlegm. Each cough would resonate as if you had virtually pulled on that blanket of skin. Now put your hand on your stomach and press it and cough. You don't feel as much pain. That's why heart patients often squeeze a pillow on their stomachs to ease the necessary but painful experience of coughing after open heart surgery. The coughing experience is so painful that many heart patients would regularly "forget" to cough up their phlegm or cough it up only perfunctorily without earning the full health benefit.

Now the teddy bear/pillow is a friendly reminder of the need for patients to cough up their phlegm or risk serious infection. Sir Cough-a-Lot is a visible reminder of the need for the patient to give the teddy bear a squeeze every so often. And of course Sir Cough-a Lot- readily catches the attention of the visiting grandchildren and consistently serves as a conversation starter for the patient and his and her family. Consider another innovative example that turned the ordinary into something extra- ordinary with no additional resources. That innovation begins when an 18-year old walks past a construction site. He sees a foundation and cellar under construction for a large building. He notices the dirt being hauled away is a kind of clay that could be valuable as a cleaning powder to take grease out of wool clothing. So he has the bluish clay dirt delivered to his home where he pressed it and packaged it and sold $6,000 worth of the clay cakes. Six years later, Charles Hires would leverage that same sense of resourcefulness in founding Hires Root Beer in 1876 — 10 years before Coca-Cola (1886) and 17 years before Pepsi-Cola (1893).

Improvising leaders can turn scraps into masterpieces:

1. Who says you have to use a full 8 1/2 by 11 page of paper to write a book? Not an improvising leader like John Burke. He wrote *The Pilgrim's Progress* on untwisted papers used to cork bottles.

2. Who says you have to solve mathematical problems for others to view only on a chalk board? Not George Stephenson, the engineer who invented the locomotive. He wrote his mathematics problems with chalk on the sides of grimy coal wagons.

Go ahead. Be a leader. And squeeze innovation out of teddy bear and find something new in what you thought you knew.

Today's ImproveMINT

*Look for substitute resources
to keep your leadership thinking in mint condition.*

●

Mint 15

Breaking Out of Perception Prison

Reading time: 3:35

One night at sea, a ship's captain saw what looked like the lights of another ship heading toward him on a collision course. He had his signalman blink to the other ship: "Change your course 10 degrees south." The reply came back, "Change YOUR course 10 degrees north." The ship's captain answered, "I'm a full captain — change your course south." To which the reply was, "Well, I'm a seaman first class, change your course north." This insubordination infuriated the captain, so he signaled back, "Dammit, I say change your course south. I'm in a battleship." To which the reply came, "And I say change your course north. I'm in a lighthouse."

Stephen Covey, the author of *Principle-Centered Leadership* and *The 7 Habits of Highly Effective People,* closed many of his leadership seminars with that true story. And in the process he helped future leaders break out of their personal prisons of perception and helped each of them become a more adept leader. The Battleship vs. Lighthouse story helps us more fully embrace William James' observation that whenever two people meet there are really six people present. James said there is:

1.   Each person as s/he sees herself/himself
2.   Each person as the other person sees her or him.
3.   Each person as he or she really is.

Let's examine that power of perception. Let's turn the clock back to the late 1890s. You're a cowboy in the American West. You're viewing your first "picture-show," your first movie — a western. Suddenly the bad guys on the screen start shooting. They seem so life-like, so real, and so deadly. Instinctively, you reach for your gun and do what comes naturally to a gun-wielding cowboy: you start shooting at the bad guys on the screen. Historians tell us this earlier version of the Battleship vs. Lighthouse story happened often. And why not? Responding to gunfire is the modus operandi of a cowboy. It comes with the territory. Those cowboys in the theater were only defending themselves. Those cowboys shooting at a movie screen remind us of Plato's observation that we are trapped inside a cave and know the world only through the shadows it casts on the wall. (Or a movie screen).

And those shadows vary according to the time of day, as author John Steinbeck observed in his novel *Travels with Charley.* He wrote: "So much there is to see but our morning eyes describe a different world than do our afternoon eyes, and surely our wearied afternoon eyes can only report a weary evening world." That's why the most effective leaders bring a 360 degree perspective to their vision no matter what time of day. As Marcel Proust observed: "The real act of discovery consists not in finding new lands but in seeing with new eyes." New eyes that could discern there are 293 different ways to change a dollar bill with common coins. Leaders might even subscribe to the observation of a nine year-old as she sipped a soft drink through a straw: "Too bad I don't have eyes in my mouth." Leaders do. They have virtual eyes everywhere. They have eyes that help them better filter out the light that if left unattended could blind their judgment. They have eyes that help them focus on their particular expertise. And they have eyes that scan their pertinent experience to better discern the situation and more realistically align the strategic intent before jumping to a conclusion that's obvious. And wrong. Even if you're in a battleship.

Today's ImproveMINT

Break out of your Perception Prison
to keep your leadership thinking in mint condition.

●

Mint 16

Where You Stand Depends Where You Sit

Reading time: 3:44

Her five-year-old granddaughter was very inquisitive. She wanted to know her grandmother's age. "Old enough to know better," the grandmother would say dismissively. Or she would joke like Phyllis Diller: "So old that my back goes out more often than I do." But then one day the 60-month old seemed to get the best of the 60-year-old. "Grandma, I know how old you are."

"You do?" her grandma wondered. "Yes it's right here," the little girl said as she spilled the contents of her grandma's purse on the floor. "I see your birth date right there," the precocious little girl said pointing to the grandma's driver's license. "And grandma, I see that you were not a very good student, no, no, no." "I wasn't?" the grandma asked incredulously. "No, no, no. See you got an F." "An F!" the grandmother exclaimed. "Yes look at that F....in SEX," the little girl said. They both laughed.

No matter how many times you've heard that well-traveled story in business circles of yesteryear, the critical insight is still relevant: perception is the reality. Yet how many leaders really take the time to look at problems from other points of view? After all, where you stand on an issue depends on where you sit. If you are pursuing a Great White Whale, you will see white as bleakly as did Herman Melville, the author of *Moby Dick*. In pursuit of the Great White Whale, Melville's perception of white became not a color but "the absence of all colors—a dumb blankness."

Where you stand on an issue depends on where you sit. If you were Hawaiian natives in the 1700s and you eyed British explorer John Cook's boats, you were not looking for transportation. You saw those boats as so many fish hooks. The nails that kept the boat together were more valuable to the natives than the boat itself. After all, those natives lived thousands of miles away from the iron mills that produced fish hooks and other tools.

Where you stand on an issue depends on where you sit. If you were sitting in a jungle, you would have laughed at anyone who told you that fire was deadly—even Albert Schweitzer. The natives saw fire from a much different point of view. The natives quite literally slept with fires in their huts to ward off the mosquitoes. Dr. Schweitzer saw the fires as a safety hazard. But the natives knew the high humidity in the jungle would keep fires from spreading. Indeed, where you stand on an issue depends on where you sit.

So next time you are developing strategic direction and/or policy, FIRST step into the shoes of your followers. See the "facts" as they see them. From their point of view, from their reference point. To the 5-year-old, the "facts" of her grandma's birth date and sex were clear and their meaning evident. At least from her POV —Point of View.

Indeed, it takes a leader to step back and better refine if not define reality. Then the most effective leaders figuratively step into someone else shoes to see what they see from their point of view. Or else they risk getting an "F." In leadership.

Today's ImproveMINT

Be aware of other points of view
to keep your leadership thinking in mint condition.

●

Lighten Up
& Enlighten Yourself

Reading time: 3:38

M oaning and groaning in my losing battle with the flu bug, I blurted out in pain one early morning. "Oh, God. Oh, God!" I moaned. And moaned. My wife, lying next to me, sized up the situation quickly. She knew I was looking more for sympathy than for survival. "Oh, God. Oh God!" I moaned again. "Yes" deadpanned my wife right on cue. "How can I help you?" I laughed. The more I laughed the more I hurt. Oh, my aching ribs. But I didn't care. It was funny. And I laughed — at the hurt. My wife's sense of humor taught me a lesson in what I have come to understand as the FUNdamentals of Leadership. That's the uncanny ability of leaders to use comic relief in real or perceived tense situations to renew, revive and rekindle the heart and soul of others. After all, FUNdamental Leadership breaks down barriers.

Consider the way George H. Bush, then sitting president of the United States, tapped into his sense of self-deprecating humor to make a stronger connection to his audience in Chicago. Bush, the titular head of the free world, said he knew the audience wanted to hear a few words from a prominent figure who can really fire up a crowd. "Unfortunately, Bears coach Mike Ditka is getting ready for next week's game and (my wife) Barbara Bush couldn't make it either, so here I am." When Ronald Reagan was 73, the President of the United States used humor to chastise those who thought he was too old to run for a second term. His opponent was nearly 20 years younger. Reagan said: "I will not exploit for political purposes my opponent's youth and inexperience." Even his opponent laughed. And so did Reagan —and millions of Americans—

all the way to the ballot box and onto another political victory woven in part with the threads of humor. Your sense of humor—your FUNdamentals of Leadership—can also foment productivity, according to a study conducted at California State University. People who said their jobs were satisfying and a lot of fun were more productive than those who said their jobs were satisfying but not a lot of fun. They used their sense of humor to displace their anger as Sigmund Freud once defined humor. Your sense of humor, your displaced anger, your FUNdamentals of Leadership can enhance your creativity. "Ha, ha is the first cousin of Aha," writes Michael Gelb in his book: *Thinking for a Change*. Humor broadens our perspective. As Rev. Billy Graham said humor helps us:

"...overlook the unbecoming,
understand the unconventional,
tolerate the unpleasant,
overcome the unexpected and
outlast the unbearable."

No wonder the most effective leaders use their sense of humor to ease tension and shrug off the burden of embarrassment as Bob Dole demonstrated during his presidential campaign. The World War II decorated veteran fell off a platform in front of the media and an enthusiastic audience. His FUNdamentals of leadership well-honed, he got up, smiled and quipped: "I think I just earned my third Purple Heart (the medal awarded to those wounded or killed serving in the US military)."

Indeed, humor broadens the mind to new perspectives, new learnings, new opportunities. Humor clarifies the important, chastises the ignorant and even unmasks the delinquent plying and lying for attention. "Oh God!"

Today's ImproveMINT

Lighten Up. Hone your sense of humor
to keep your leadership thinking in mint condition.

●

Mint 18

E-Quip Yourself
With Humor
Reading time: 3:13

Nancy Reagan, criticized for her royal taste in expensive china and designer clothes, defended her shopping sprees and noted that she was not acting like a queen. "After all a tiara would surely muss my hair," the former First Lady responded to reporters with her tongue firmly wedged in her cheek.   President Ronald Reagan, shrugging off criticism of his age as the oldest elected president, told reporters with a twinkle in his eye and a smirk on his face: "Thomas Jefferson once said, 'We should never judge a president by his age, only by his works.' And ever since he told me that, I stopped worrying."

Ah, the art of the self-effacing quip. It's a skill that the most effective leaders wield to turn stress into something less and blunt sharpened personality clashes in the workplace. Consider the particularly hard-charging stallion of a leader who had ruffled more than a few feathers on his team. He opened a staff meeting in silence. He merely projected a photo of a stunning horse grazing in a meadow. Then the leader simply looked up admiringly at the photo. Then 20 seconds later he broke his silence, saying "I don't think anybody here disagrees that I am a real workhorse." He paused, looked around the room at his team and added: "The problem is that maybe we don't all agree on which end I am!" His team laughed at the self-effacing humor of their leader. His horse's-ass inference broke the tension "primarily because he showed some real vulnerability and some understanding of how his staff perceives him," according to one team member at that staff meeting. Then his team participated in a more productive meeting with a few laughs still ringing in their ears. Ah, the art of the self-effacing quip. Consider the no-nonsense leader who seemed to storm into work on a mission one morning without regard to anyone and anything else. A colleague confronted the leader: "I heard from a few folks that you were having a rough day today. Are you okay? The tightly wound leader smiled. She quipped: "Everything is fine today. I parked my broom in the parking lot like always and made doubly sure I did my finger nails extra long and sharp today." Her self-effacing humor underscored her emotional intelligence in seeing herself as other see her. She also reinforcing her sense of self-confidence and self-esteem to be open to criticism that would ultimately enhance her leadership effectiveness.

Ah, the art of the quip can also be used to turn a lemon of a situation into proverbial lemonade. A college professor walked into to a lecture hall and found that his students had moved out all the chairs. The professor put down his notes, looked up and said triumphantly: "Thank you for that standing ovation, amazing there's so much interest in my talk tonight that every seat in the house is taken." Victor Borge, the comedian pianist, opened his show and noticed that half of the seats were unsold. Nonplussed, Borge deadpanned: "This must be a very rich audience. I see each of you have purchased two or three seats." A subscriber called to complain of a live spider crawling around inside his newspaper. The editor (Mark Twain) said the spider took up "temporary residence in the newspaper because it was looking for what merchants were NOT advertising in the newspaper. That way the spider could go to those stores who were not advertising, spin his web across the door and lead a life undisturbed." Smile more than defile. Do what leaders do: E-quip yourself with humor.

Today's ImproveMINT

E-Quip yourself with a sense of humor
to keep your leadership thinking in mint condition.

●

Mint 19

The Wall Street Journal. Period.

Reading time: 3:19

How embarrassing! After all, I had been reading The Wall Street Journal for years. Then one day I noticed –for the first time--that large PERIOD punctuation mark in the masthead. How could I miss something THAT evident? *The Wall Street Journal.* That period has been there for more than 100 years, including the eight years that I had been reading the business-of-business publication. That big black period stared me right in the face day after day, week after week, month after month, year after year. And I didn't even notice! Scary. I felt so incompetent as a leader. I always thought of myself more apt to notice and respond to information from a variety of sources and formats, especially a source with that high degree of definitiveness. But I missed this period. Period! No excuses. And I felt more inept than adept. I know it may seem like just a little dot to most of you but that little dot loomed like a mountain of mistakes to me because I missed a clear piece of data -- at my fingertips! I had assumed that *The Wall Street Journal's* masthead conformed to all other newspaper mastheads I had read. And so my eyesight lacked insight.

But I learned my lesson, a leadership lesson. I learned to become more strategic and sensitive to input: to see more than simply observe and to listen more rather than simply hear. And I learned to play Scrabble with a more discerning eye that in part helped me become a more cognizant leader. (Stay with me here even though this sounds weird.) I devised a little word game to spur my powers of perception. I did not want to make the mistake again of not completely reading something right in front of me. So I deliberately studied very familiar words that I regularly overlooked — at first glance. I forced myself to find a very visible, very accessible yet "hidden" meaning within the word much like that period hid from me right out in the open. Let's play: Consider these three unrelated words: block, danger, and climb.

If you're like me, you didn't see the word within the word—at first glance anyway — THE word that more fully develops a stronger relationship between the two words. Let's review:

- You read: BLOCK. The first time I read that word—BLOCK— I didn't readily see the word LOCK in Block or make the connection that a lock is used to block someone's access.

- You read: DANGER. The first time I read that word—DANGER— I didn't readily see the word ANGER in Danger or make the connection that anger can be a reaction to danger.

- You read: CLIMB. The first time I read that word —CLIMB—I didn't readily see the word LIMB in Climb or make the connection that you climb a limb.

After playing that little word-within-a-word game, you know more fully than ever before that the devil is in the details. Now you are even more aware that the word— EVIL—is in the word Devil. But the most effective leaders don't need word games to stimulate their thinking on a regular basis. They are more apt to read data more critically, to focus on the messaging more intentionally and to more accurately read the front of page of The Wall Street Journal. PERIOD.

Today's ImproveMINT

***Stay vigilant reviewing familiar information
to keep your leadership thinking in mint condition.***

●

Mint 20

Smelling the ROSE
Of Creativity

Reading time: 2:28.

Climbing into the car after a long day at school, the 6-year-old boy flung his head outside the window into the 55-mile-an-hour wind. His mother yanked the little boy back in the car, and chided: "What do you think you're doing, Mister?

The boy said matter-of-factly: "I'm airing out my brains. My brain got dusty today with all that math."

Is your brain a bit dusty too?

Well, today let's collectively roll down the windows to air out our brains. And with each of the four windows we roll down, let's smell the ROSE of creativity. ROSE is an acrostic for four windows you can roll down to air out the cobwebs in your brain and strengthen your creative leadership:

Reverse

Opposite

Sequence

Enterprise

REVERSE

What would happen if the roles were reversed: What if students graded teachers? And what if employees graded bosses? What if employees became customers? What if a doctor became a patient? What if a prison warden became a prisoner for a day?

OPPOSITE

What would happen if what is true was no longer true? Then you have to focus on the opposite like this: 3M product researcher Arthur Fry focused on the opposite when he invented glue that didn't stick very well. He invented the highly successful Post It notes.

SEQUENCE

What would happen if the usual sequence of events was changed? What if a birthday candle lit AFTER you blew it out? What if you were given a baseball uniform BEFORE you made the team? What if you painted your house before it was built? What if you paid for your college education 15 years before you started?

ENTERPRISE

What would happen if basketballs didn't need air? What would happen if everyone learned a second language before they were 12 years old? What would happen if you visited a bargain book store. Blindly reach into the discounted sales bin of books. Choose a book and don't look at it until you get back to the office or home. Or consider window shopping in stores you have never been in before. Then, selectively wander in and around. Look for items you have never even thought of looking for before.

Today's ImproveMINT

Dust off the cobwebs in your brain every so often to keep your leadership thinking in mint condition.

Mint 21

Height Insight:
Attitude Not Altitude

Reading time: 3:35

She's the leader of a multimillion dollar foundation. Smart. Witty. And 3-feet-9 inches tall. She deals with community and business leaders with a commanding sense of authority. Her leadership skill is evident and her leadership lesson is clear: your self-confidence is a measure of your attitude not your altitude, an attitude of respect and empathy for others. Consider William Seward, a 5-foot-6 senator from New York. He ran in the 1860 Republican Primary against 6-foot-4 Abraham Lincoln. Historian Doris Kearns Goodwin, in her book *Team of Rivals*, says that Seward nevertheless was a "commanding figure, an outsized personality against whom larger men seemed smaller." How do vertically-challenged leaders seem taller? The most effective leaders, regardless of their height, are curious about others and let criticism roll off their backs. That's what Seward did. Again quoting Doris Kearns Goodwin:

> *"Seward was genuinely interested in people, curious about their families and the smallest details of their lives, anxious to help with their problems. As a public man, he possessed unusual resilience, enabling him to accept criticism with good humored serenity."*

Being able to accept criticism requires a high–degree of authenticity (being comfortable in your own skin) and competency. That's why how well you do your job means a lot more than how well-to-do you are as a physical specimen extraordinaire. Indeed competency is the key to seeming taller. As one researcher on height observed, "Qualifications, experience and charm will do much more for one's job prospects than a pair of stilettos." The history books prove that height insight. Consider the measure of these world leaders: Standing 5-feet tall: Israel's Ben Gurion and China's Deng Xiaoping. Standing 5-feet-3: Palestine's Liberation Organization's Yasser Yarafat, India's Mahatma Gandhi, North Korea's Kim Jong-il, Jordan's King Hussein, Soviet Union's Nikita Kruschef and Russia's Dmtry Medvedev. Standing 5-feet-6: Japan's Emperor Hirohito, France's Nicolas Sarkozy, Soviet Union's Joseph Stalin and Great Britain's Admiral Horatio Nelson. At 5 feet, French engineer Gustave Eiffel wasn't too vertically challenged to build the 1,061-foot tall Eiffel Tower in Paris. At 5–feet 2 inches Napoleon wasn't too vertically challenged to become Emperor of France and conqueror of the world. At 5 feet 3 inches, Desmond Tutu wasn't too vertically challenged to fight apartheid in South Africa. At 5 feet 4 inches, James Madison wasn't too vertically challenged to serve as President of the United States, Father of the Constitution, author of the Bill of Rights and a co-author of the Federalist Papers. At 5 feet 5 inches, magician Harry Houdini wasn't too vertically challenged to become the Great Escape Artist. And at 5 feet 6 inches Benjamin Harrison and Martin Van Buren weren't too vertically challenged to serve as Presidents of the United States.

Indeed, there can be great strength in less length. X-rays are light waves that are 1,000 times shorter than visible light. Yet X-rays are strong enough to burrow through your flesh. And medical technicians will tell you the shorter the acoustic wavelength, the sharper the sonogram picture. Less is more. In car racing, the shorter the sound wave, the louder the race car roars by the grand stand. In playing the harp's 47 strings ranging from 3-inches to 60-inches, the shorter the string, the higher the pitch. And the shorter (smaller) the bubbles the better tasting the champagne.

Today's ImproveMINT

Supersize your leadership with an interest in others to keep your leadership thinking in mint condition.

Are You Too Good To Get Better?

Reading time: 2:58

You were the top sales person on your team. Just a few weeks ago. Or you were the most prolific accountant in the department. Just a few weeks ago. Or you were _____, fill in the blank. Just a few weeks ago. And now you are losing sales, missing project deadlines and making too many mistakes. You are losing it. What worked yesterday fails today. You're stunned. You're frustrated. You're embarrassed. You shout in exasperation: "How could this have happened to me? Then later in the confines of your vehicle — alone on your commute home — you scream to your windshield: "I am good at what I do. Just look at my record. I am Good! Good! Good!"

Maybe too good.

You're so good at it that you gradually become bad at it. When you get too good at something you may stop trying to get better at it. Or worse: you start bypassing the basics. Been there. Done that. And you veer off the road to success you've navigated so well for so long.

Enantiodromia

That's why the most effective leaders guard against *enantiodromia* – a Greek word that means "the ability of anything followed UNTHINKINGLY to turn into its exact opposite." Your punch list is intact. You think you're so good at what you do that you don't have to go methodically step by step. You're too quick to jump from A to D then even quicker to jump to P. That "I-know-it-all" strength can then ironically deteriorate into your "I-am-falling-apart" weakness. Your expertise can become your expertease. Your helpful, understanding and compassionate expertise can become your self-serving, selective and narrow-minded expertease. All show and no dough. All hat and no horse. That's why the most effective leaders guard against their strength becoming their weakness. Leaders leverage continuous learning to keep what's fresh today from going stale tomorrow. As David E. Kelley, the founder of IDEO, observes: *"There is incremental improvement to anything. The only reason we stop creating is that we run out of time or budget."*

That's why the most effective and continuously improving leaders marshal their curiosity. They are bitten by a need to know something new — not smitten with what they already knew. They rely less on their years of experience and more on their ears of coherence. They listen and learn. They look first for the chinks in their own armor no matter how well-polished. They parlay the good they are doing today into doing even better tomorrow. But how do you sharpen your expertise when you already think you are the sharpest tool in the shed? How do you guard against *enantiodromia*? Go back to the basics, no matter how seasoned you are, no matter how many accolades you have and no matter how many bonus checks you've cashed. Become vigilant like legendary professional football coach Vince Lombardi who surprised his Green Bay Packers— veteran players with 15-20 years experience playing football. Lombardi intoned: "Gentlemen: This is a football." He held the ball high in the air like a trophy. That was like demonstrating a scalpel to a surgeon or fire hose to a fire fighter or bible to a minister. Yet his back-to-basics posture paid off. Lombardi and his Green Bay Packers won the first two Super Bowls. As leaders, they warded off that dreaded *enantiodromia*. With expertise not expertease.

Today's ImproveMINT:

Keep looking for chinks in your own armor
to keep your leadership thinking in mint condition.

●

Mint 23

Broadening Your Funnel Vision

Reading time: 2:54

E ager to show off his newly learned arithmetic skills, the first grader stood up and blurted out the answer: "Four!" The teacher had just posed this question:

> *"If there were five birds in a tree and you shot one of them with your slingshot, how many birds would be left?"*

Proud of getting the answer first, the boy sat back down. And thought. A few seconds later, he stood back up and blurted out a correction: "None!"

In those few seconds of second thoughts, the young boy demonstrated that he could think strategically. He could define, align and evaluate the factors. He could discern, dissect and determine the facts affecting the situation. In those few seconds of second thoughts, the young boy discerned the context as much as the content of the problem. And in those few seconds of second thoughts, the young boy grasped the consequence of his decision: all the birds would be scared off by a single shot.

That's what the most effective leaders do. They grasp the consequences of their thinking beyond the sequence of their actions. They turn ordinary sequential tunnel vision into an extra-ordinary consequential Funnel Vision to embrace a wider array of factors that affect their decisions. That's why the most effective leaders are wary of getting trapped in their own tunnel vision where the right decision seems so evident and ultimately so wrong. They know how easy it is to make what appears to be the right decision in the wrong context. They know how easy it is to be more righteous than right and end up woefully wrong. Consider Dr. Ferdinand Porsche locked in his own tunnel vision. He made what he thought was the right decision on Hitler's orders in World War II. Porsche designed the world's largest, strongest, and most durable tank. But the 180-ton tank with 9-inch steel plating sank on the dirt roads.

Indeed, the context is as critical as the content in making effective decisions. Consider another example where context trumped the content of a decision that major league baseball officials made building the world's first multi-purposed domed sports stadium. The lighting glare off the translucent roof at the now defunct Houston Astrodome proved dangerous. Outfielders had to wear protective helmets. And the solution –painting the roof to curb the glare—created another problem. The grass on the field died without adequate light. Finally, when baseball officials in Houston broadened their tunnel vision into more strategic Funnel Vision, they gave birth to a more creative, more strategic solution to solve both the lighting glare and the grass dying problems at the same time. Those officials sparked the invention of AstroTurf—artificial grass.

The leadership lesson is clear: Broaden your Funnel Vision to see your problem from a more strategic point of view so that you can spawn more apt solutions. Blurting out the first thing that comes to your mind can be counter-productive, especially when you only have one shot no matter how many birds you're facing.

Today's ImproveMINT

Broaden your Funnel Vision
to keep your leadership thinking in mint condition.

●

Mint 24

Problem-Solving At 250 Miles Per Hour

Reading time: 3:46

You're all set to dig into that juicy steak grilling on a beautiful summer day when suddenly you hear BZZZZZZZZZZZZZZZZZZ SLAP! Stung by a bee. Oh, it hurts. You probably just winced at the thought of a bee sting. Oh, the power in a painful bee sting. But the power in the brain of a honey bee is even more amazing. The honey bee can perform 50 different thinking acts that require memorizing or predicting. Memorizing: The bee memorizes the location of five different flowerbeds. Predicting: The bee predicts the exact hour that each of those flowers come into bloom. All of that ingenuity with a brain the size of a grain of sugar. Now if a brain the size of a grain of sugar can do all that, imagine the power in a brain the size of a grapefruit—the human brain.

The most effective leaders leverage the significance and scope of the human brain that is 100,000 times larger than the brain of a bee and packs 10 million times more cells for a total of 10 billion cells. Imagine 10 billion cells in your brain rocking, rolling and rattling around between your ears to help you lead in especially challenging times. Ten billion cells! How much is 10 billion? Well if you counted one cell per second, it would take you 320 years to count to 10 billion. Scientists tell us your brain flashes 100,000 chemical reactions every second. Your brain ignites 60,000 thoughts every single day and fires messages at 250 miles per hour. And when it comes to (stored) memory, your brain can challenge any computer. Researchers tell us that in a 70-year-lifetime, you will be able to store enough information in your brain to fill the entire 32,000 page Encyclopedia Britannica 500,000 times. Your memory capacity is so intricately woven together that if you stretched all the gray matter in your brain from end to end, it would reach 8,000 miles. No wonder one researcher called the brain —The Enchanted Loom —a loom capable of weaving those 8,000 miles of thinking threads into a variety of quilt-like patterns of robust thought too intricate and extensive to count. Meanwhile the complex construction of your body's DNA, blood vessels, and muscles in support of the brain are equally as awesome. That's why the most effective leaders embrace William Shakespeare's observation in *Hamlet*: "What a piece of work is a man! How noble in reason, how infinite in faculty, how admirable in action." And how magnificent in composition!

- So magnificent that if the human body's DNA material could be uncoiled, it would stretch from the earth to the sun —AND BACK—1,000 times, according to the *Body Almanac* by Neil McAleer.
- So magnificent that your body is honeycombed with 60,000 miles of blood vessels — enough to stretch twice around the world.
- So magnificent your heart will pump 56 million gallons of blood in a 72-year lifetime — enough to fill the tanks of more than 2,000 Boeing 747 jets!
- So magnificent that if all 639 of the body's muscles were pulling in the same direction, you would have the equivalent of 25 tons of pulling power.

And so magnificent that a single red blood cell can travel 950 miles in four months —the equivalent of a human traveling 80,000 times around the earth (two billion miles). Busier than any bee.

Today's ImproveMINT

Appreciate the awesome power of your brain
to keep your leadership thinking in mint condition.

●

Beware of Jumping to Conclusions

Reading time: 3:24

Pull the toggle! Pull the toggle! Pull the toggle! The commands blared over my two-way radio as I hung from my parachute 3,000 feet over South Florida. It was my first parachute jump. My jump instructor on the ground screamed at me to steer my parachute for a safe landing by pulling the toggle. I pulled. I pulled. And I pulled. The more I pulled, the louder the commands blared on the radio buckled into my chest. No wonder the jump instructor was infuriated. I was off course and heading for a nightmare of a landing. I looked down. There were electrical power high-tension wires immediately below me, a canal just in front of me and a wooded area to the left of me. "Pull the toggle! Pull the toggle! Pull the toggle!" I pulled. My steering "wheel" seemed locked. I was drifting down to a terrible landing. And I was scared.

Suddenly the horizon began to rise on me. And thud. I landed. Not in the canal. Not in the wires. Not in the woods. I landed in a cornfield. More than a mile off target. "Why didn't you pull the toggle when I told you to?" demanded my flight instructor after climbing through the tall corn field to rescue me. "Look it is as simple as this." He pulled the small handle on the steering line. Then I realized my mistake, a mistake that almost got me killed, and a mistake that I had trained for at least three hours to avoid. In my excitement dangling at 3,000 feet, I grabbed the harness rope instead of grasping the steering toggle a few inches farther from me.

Are you like me? Sometimes grabbing what is handy instead of grasping what would be more dandy to your well-being. And ultimately failing to really get a grip. Too many would-be leaders are impulsively grabbing what they CAN instead of really grasping what they SHOULD. And then we end up in potentially embarrassing situations. Consider the newspaper headline that read: FDR (President Franklin Delano Roosevelt) in Bed with Coed. Ooops. It should have read "in bed with COLD." Consider the story published in a newsletter on a consultant who said she had to be flexible on her FEE. Ooops. She actually said "on her feet."

Effective leaders know how impotent they can be when they blindly follow one another around in endless circles like those circling caterpillars of French naturalist Jean Henri Fabre. Those caterpillars marched around and around in a procession to their death. They unknowingly starved to death even though food was just inches away. They blindly followed each other to nowhere. Like me during my parachute descent, those caterpillars were involved but not engaged, passionate but not purposeful and focused but not truly aimed.

The leadership lesson is clear: Focusing means a lot more than keeping your eyes open and grabbing the first thing you see. Pull the toggle!

Today's ImproveMINT:

Rein in your impulsive thinking
to keep your leadership thinking in mint condition.

●

Mint 26

Narrowing Your Attention Span

Reading time: 4:01

Hank Aaron became baseball's all-time home run hitter — a record he held for 33 years until 2007— with the help of a well-developed ritual that narrowed and sharpened his attention span. After swinging a bat in the on-deck circle, Aaron would take off his baseball cap. Then he would narrow his focus looking through one of the small holes (air vents) in his cap at the pitcher. The small holes helped Aaron more carefully frame his view, fix his attention and filter out distractions to better prepare to meet the pending challenge in the batter's box. Narrowing our attention spans and focusing enough to separate the wheat from the chaff is a critical leadership skill especially against the flood of information that flows into and out of our attention spans like a Flood of Facebook Likes or Tsunami of Tweets and Texts. Too much too fast. With a narrowed attention span comes enhanced precision and performance.

How narrow do you focus your full attention? As narrow as an arrow. You might recall the Hindu story of the Master Archer who is teaching a student to hit the target — a bird made out of a straw hung from a tree. "What do you see?" asks the master of the first student. "The tree and the bird, the bow and the arrow, my arm and you," the student answers. The master dismisses the student. A second student is summoned, "What do you see?" the master asks. "I see a bird," the student says. "Describe the bird," the master insists. "I can't," says the student. "I see only his neck." The master gives the student permission to shoot. The tighter the focus the better the performance. How do you tighten your focus? How do you narrow your attention span? Exercise your Veranda Rights. Envision yourself settling into your rocking chair on a warm summer afternoon in a small mid-Western town at the turn of the 20th century. As you rock away on your veranda, time always slows down and thinking always speeds up. Your thinking is broader and more contemplative when you exercise your Veranda Rights. You slow down and think of more creative options. You resist reacting to the problem de jour in *Whackamo* fashion where you quickly address one issue before the next issue pops up and grabs your attention.

Exercising Your
Veranda Rights

Veranda Rights can do for leadership what Miranda Rights have done for justice. In administering Miranda Rights, arresting officers must notify people of their right to remain silent or have their attorney present during police questioning. *"You have the right to remain silent. Anything you say can and will be used against you in a court of law…"* That Miranda Rights warning serves to cool down a volatile situation so that cooler heads can prevail and both sides of an issue can be addressed equally. Then you can more strategically narrow your attention span. In narrowing your attention span, think of yourself like the homeowner closing off heating vents in certain rooms to funnel the same amount of heat into an even smaller, more concentrated, and more focused space. Have you ever noticed that the warmest room in your house is the smallest (narrowest)? Make room for that kind of limited focus to warm your thinking. Then maybe your decision-making will be so blessed, so focused as you exercise your Veranda Rights that you won't have to wear a "holy" hat.

Today's ImproveMINT

Narrow your focus to keep
your leadership thinking in mint condition.

●

Mint 27

Creation Out Of Devastation

Reading time: 3:09

O kay you screwed up. The team you led finished way out of the money. Your leadership is being questioned —mostly by you. You feel lousy. Your get-up-and-go got-up-and-went. Now, the only thing you can lead is a scream. And it seems you'll never stop wiping the embarrassment off your face. How do you bounce back from feeling that bad, from feeling that burned out?

You might find some relief in thinking about how burned out the Great American Prairie was more than 300 years ago, a burning devastation that led to a blossoming celebration. Wildfires would inevitably and ironically lead to the creation of vibrant wildflowers. The concept of wildflowers-out-of-wildfires underscores the credence of Pablo Picasso's observation that: "Every act of creation is first of all an act of destruction." Indeed Picasso could have been referring to the Great American Prairie as an example of creation out of devastation. Long before the onslaught of highways and high-rises, cattle and corn, the Great Prairie rose across America like so many phoenixes rising up from the ashes. The Great American Prairie rose healthier and heartier BECAUSE OF the charred devastation often ignited by lightning.

Historians tell us the lightning-sparked burning process impregnated the soil with a surge of acidity that ironically stimulated the growing capacity of the vast land. Those wildfires burned weeds, spurned clutter and churned a revitalized growth. In fact, wildfires flamed the prairie into a 250 million-acre cauldron bubbling with colorful wildflowers that spilled over the land. Chances are you too have wildflowers lying dormant in the Soil of Your Soul. Your wildflowers –your creative ideas–could blossom with the same vim and vigor that blossomed those wildflowers buried deep in your blackened soul.

So the next time you screw up and go down in virtual flames, think of the essence of your personal leadership as versatile and vibrant as the prairie, where the wildflowers (new ideas) in them, can burst through the suffocating blackened ash (of failed projects) and shower a spectrum of colorful solutions that brighten the day and heighten the way. Indeed, resilient and resourceful leaders think of themselves as vibrant, vast and varied as a prairie:

- Where their scope is not limited
- Where their goals are not confined
- Where their dreams have room to roam
- Where their creative spirit is born to be wild

No matter how much the naysayers try to harness a leader's zeal or burn out a leader's vision.

Today's ImproveMINT

Turn devastation into the creation of a fresh start to keep your leadership thinking in mint condition.

Washing Away
the Dregs

Reading time: 2:56

Are you smarter than a fifth grader? Turns out I'm about as smart as a third grader. At least in this case. My only consolation is that these third graders introduced me to a creative and innovative leader who helped me learn a key leadership lesson: the importance of uncovering hidden resources— especially those hidden in plain view. Of course, these were no ordinary third graders. No these were The Third Graders at a North Carolina elementary school who challenged Nabisco's claim that their Chips Ahoy package of chocolate chip cookies had more than 1,000 chocolate chips in each bag. The students counted only 340 to 680 chocolate chips.

I counted 671.

Feeling cheated out of their chocolate chips, The Third Graders shared their collective concern in a letter to the company. In response to that letter, Nabisco sent a food technician — a Ph.D. —to visit the school in Wadesboro. The expert would count the chips in a new bag of Chips Ahoy chocolate chip cookies in front of all the students. Before counting the chocolate chips, the Nabisco leader first washed away all the cookie dough from the chocolate chips. Then the Nabisco leader discovered the cold hard fact: the students were right! There weren't 1,000 chocolate chips in the Chips Ahoy bag.

No, there were exactly 1,181 chocolate chips!

And I wondered how many thinking chips I had still hidden in my brain—thinking chips that were barricaded and blocked in my brain, thinking chips still covered with the dough in my life clogging my ability to problem-solve with greater utility. What if I had more HIDDEN resources between my ears or at the tips of my fingers that were still there for the taking — resources hidden deep within me like a buried treasure? What if I could uncover that ability to think with greater clarity? What if I could recover hidden resources in me? The questions kept swirling through my mind. Maybe I didn't have all the answers but those Third Graders got me thinking. And they helped me learn a valuable leadership lesson: Before trying to solve a problem, cleanse your thinking. Wash away the dregs. Clear away the clutter. After all, no one ever paints a fence or a wall without first washing away all the dirt on it.

Now whenever I am facing a problem I first step back. I take a deep breath. I try to clear my head of all the clutter. I try to wash away all that dough clogging my brain with so many chants of "No, You Can't." And I look for the portals of opportunity, the proverbial pony in the pile of manure that just has to be in there somewhere. Then I can leverage the most creative use of all my resources to make an even more productive strategic decision—the kind you can count on. And let the cookie crumble where it may.

Today's ImproveMINT

Cleanse your thinking
to keep your leadership thinking in mint condition.

●

Mint 29

Reach Out & Touch
the Face of a New Idea
Reading time: 3:28

A lbert Einstein, as an energetic 16-year-old, climbed an 8,000-foot mountain in the Swiss Alps. There on top of Mount Santis, Einstein stood amazed —and almost in a daze — at the sparkling rays. There above the tree line and overlooking the clouds below, Einstein marveled at the brilliant spectacle of light — its purity and precision, its might and majesty—that captured his imagination. He wondered, "Could you run after a beam of light?" That wonder at the wild blue yonder led Einstein to virtually construct the launching pad into space travel and open the door to atomic power. Light played a crucial role in his theory of relativity. Indeed, Einstein had taken the first step toward greatness when he climbed up to a new level and gazed upon a higher horizon where light flashed somewhat differently in his eyes and gave him an innovative view of the future. The leadership lesson is clear: get a broader view on the issue at hand. Step up and beyond what you already knew to see something brand new. Be innovative.

Innovative leaders embrace the message in a poem titled *High Flight* that expresses the exhilaration and freedom of flying. The sentiments in the poem, written by a 19-year-old pilot John Gillespie Magee, Jr. are in the heart of every entrepreneur and in the soul if not on the lips of every effective leader. In the adaptation of the original poem on the next page, the last word is changed to a more secular notion than in the original. Yet the thematic intent is similar. The poem is a reminder to all leaders in piloting their problem-solving skies—a reminder to reach higher, a reminder to seek a broader horizon, a reminder to gain a more expansive perspective. Think of yourself as climbing into the cockpit of an airplane the next time you begin to solve a problem. Then as you take off you see the issues from a 360-degree perspective, the higher you fly the more expansive your 360-degree vision and the more insight you bring to bear on the problem (so that later you can better focus on the critical issue. (See page 69, Mint 26.)

Now imagine you are piloting an airplane at dawn's early light. You are so thrilled, so exhilarated, so enthralled with your feeling of flight. You are so elated creatively cruising and gliding on what feels like a magic carpet. You are so unbridled, so free from the grip of gravity, so inspired. Suddenly these words —adapted from the pilot's famous poem—erupt from your heart and soul at 10,000 feet:

Touch THE FACE
of a New Idea

Oh, slip the surly bonds of earth and dance the skies on laughter-silvered wings. Sunward, climb and join the tumbling mirth of sun-split clouds and do a hundred things you have never even dreamed of.

Wheeling, soaring and swinging high in the sunlit silence, I chase the shouting wind along and fling my eager craft through footless halls of air. I top the windswept heights with easy grace where never lark nor even eagle flew.

And there along the delirious burning blue in the sunlit silence I fly the high un-trespassed sanctity of space. Then I put out my hand and touch THE FACE of a new idea.

Today's ImproveMINT

Climb up to new heights
to keep your leadership thinking in mint condition.

●

Mint 30

Improvising When Your Cupboard Is Bare

Reading time: 3:11

P arty time. It's the July 4th holiday weekend. People flock to your house. More than expected. You run out of food. So, in a panic, you raid your refrigerator. But all you find is four-day old bread, a few eggs, Romano cheese and some Romaine lettuce. What do you do? You improvise. That's what Caesar Cardini did on Friday July 4, 1924 when his restaurant in Tijuana, Mexico ran out of food supplies. Caesar improvised with whatever he had on hand. And Caesar invented: Yep, you guessed it, Caesar salad.

Effective leaders make salad out of the proverbial parts. They improvise. They see ahead beyond what they don't have. They see ahead to what they could have. In fact the word "improvise" stems from the Latin "to see ahead." Leaders see ahead to improvise, generate new resources and broaden marketing opportunities. Caesar Cardini compensated for the lack of food supplies with his resourcefulness and showmanship. He tossed his Caesar salad in a large wooden bowl in front of the patron's table while other patrons looked on and the curiosity got the best of them. Consider the possibilities. Not the improbabilities.

Cardini, like all improvising leaders, considered the possibilities. Their mantra is to ask what if? Not what for?

Improvising leaders are more apt to look over the probabilities rather than — overlook — a hidden opportunity. Imagine you're the US Government in World War II and you're running out of gasoline. You're already rationing. How do you ask the public to ration still more gasoline, especially when people viewed the coupons as currency. Devaluing that coupon would have undermined confidence. There has to be a better way. You improvise. Instead of cutting the value of a coupon in half, you double the duration. Now a coupon would be good for a full gallon of gas every two weeks. You preserved the integrity of the value of the coupon and still cut the ration. How do you improvise like that? Try reframing your point of view. Try seeing the world the way Alexander the Great did on his 12th birthday.

His father gave him a wild horse that trainers were supposed to tame. The best trainers were called in yet none of them had any success. Alexander the Great noticed his horse seemed to be frightened of his own shadow. So during the next training session, Alexander the Great improvised. He tried something different that made a difference. He made sure his horse always faced into the sun and therefore cast no shadow. It worked. The horse was tamed and Alexander proved already as a boy that he was an improvising leader, portending that one day—21 years later—he would conquer the known world.

Alexander the Great did what improvising leaders do. They twist and turn the frame around their reality to more fully engage others in a new and more empowering vision. And together they enjoy their "salad" days of improvisation.

Today's ImproveMINT

*Repurpose whatever resources you have
to keep your leadership thinking in mint condition.*

●

Whistle While You Work

Reading time: 3:46

Screeeech! The motorist hit his brakes. Another traffic jam erupts out of nowhere. Frustrated, the motorist squeezes his fist around the steering wheel and waits for the congestion to clear up ahead. Waiting and waiting. Suddenly, he forgets all about the traffic. He finds himself singing to the radio and beating on the steering wheel as if it were a drum. And when the traffic jam cleared, the driver kept singing to himself. He didn't care that other motorists were giving him weird looks for singing his heart out. After all that music drowned out any sense of that traffic jam in his mind. Now he was figuratively dancing to his own music, reliving a memorable personal experience that music conjured up. Indeed, music has that kind of galvanizing hold on what makes us humans: our feelings, our thoughts, and our dreams.

No wonder United States Army General Norman Schwarzkopf used music to spur the can-do, will-do energy in his War Room 10 minutes before the start of The Persian Gulf War on Wednesday January 16, 1991. He called his staff together and they listened to Lee Greenwood's *God Bless the USA.* No wonder the most effective leaders embrace the power of music to galvanize the soul and focus performance. Ever notice how many 80-year-olds can easily dance to the music at a wedding but have to be helped from the dance floor to walk back to their tables? Music energizes. Maybe that's why Plato said that music was a "rhythm and harmony" that sank "deep into the caverns of the soul" and took "the strongest hold there, bringing grace to the body and mind." Music is a celebration of power like the trumpets played at horse racing tracks. Music is salutation to power like *Hail to the Chief*, signaling the entrance of the President of the United States. And music is a commemoration of power like the *Star Spangled Banner* sung before sports competitions. The record is clear on the power of music to captivate. After all, Elvis Presley twitched his lip and twirled his hips to the top of the music charts a total of 55 weeks during one 104-week span. The Beatles topped the music charts 59 times —including the five top-selling records in America—for a five-week span. And Michael Jackson's album *Thriller* sold more than 50 million copies while Pink Floyd's album *Dark Side of the Moon* sold more than 45 million copies.

No wonder the most effective leaders whistle while they work with a rhythm and a momentum that seemingly makes work fun —or at least less dreary. Think of the chants of troops on a run at boot camp. Think of the power of music so MOVING, the music could literally move large rocks to form a wall and fortify the city of Thebes, according to mythological power of Amphion's music. Myth or not, that first version of "rock n' roll" set the stage for the power of music to turn the traffic jams in our lives into jam sessions FOR our lives. So go ahead. Crank up the music. Give a "note"-worthy performance. And whistle while you work. Like a leader. With rhythm.

Today's ImproveMINT
Listen to music
to keep your leadership thinking in mint condition.

Mint 32

Off-The-Wall
Creative Thinking

Reading time: 3:14

With a sense of urgency in every step, the executive marched into the conference room. He glared at his colleagues seated for their weekly staff meeting. An eerie silence fell in the room. It was High Noon. Suddenly the executive seemed like a gunslinger, itching for some action. He flung his hand into his pocket. And he drew—a stack of index cards. Then he commanded: "STICK 'EM, UP." They did. And within a few minutes the surrounding walls were festooned with 3X5 cards and *Post-it* notes in so many colors they looked like butterflies hovering on the walls.

You know the drill. Problem solvers in an organization come together and collectively develop a list of general categories affecting the issue. Those categories are then displayed around the room either on marker boards, magnetic boards or tack-able (pin-able) boards. Then the 3X5 Index cards or *Post-it* Notes and thick marker pens are dealt to participants.

The leader challenges each person to write an idea (in less than 5 words) that would address each of the categories. The leader then asks each person to "Stick 'em up" —to stick the cards and notes on the marker board under each category. Then the participants review each other's thinking — category by category. This is where the magic of the minds comes together. This is where individuals begin to connect different ideas like so many Tinker-Toys. This is where individual threads of different ideas are collectively woven together into a thought-filled quilt of understanding and insight that no one person could have envisioned. The words on the *Post-it* Notes and Index cards take on real meaning when they are paired and compared with other ideas similarly displayed.

Those index cards can also be linked together for similar thinking or differentiated for divergent thinking. The more visual, the more information is communicated. It is particularly instructive to note that the eyes are so powerful in processing information, the nerve pathways from the eye to the brain are 25 times larger than the pathways from the ear to the brain. Thomas Edison said he could think best visually in pictures, echoing Aristotle who said the "soul never thinks without a picture." The research underscores the impact of visual communications. In his 1971 book *Silent Messages* Albert Mehrabian noted that: 55% of a message is received visually, 38% tonally and 7% vocally. (See page 217, Mint 85.)

The key in this visual off-the-wall, creative problem solving method is to view the *Post-it* Notes and Index cards like so many dots on the organization's radar screen. Then all options are open to problem solvers who are no longer locked into their own landing patterns. They have more latitude to see new connections. And when you can see all that information "flying" in/FORMATION, you never know when a "flight controller" in the room will find a new way to "stick 'em up" and land a new idea. On time. And on budget.

Today's ImproveMINT

Brainstorming sessions
keep your leadership thinking in mint condition.

●

Mint 33

Firing Up Your Personal Zamboni

Reading time: 3:25

M istakes? No problem. Just do it over. So easy. That's what you did as a kid. Why not apply the same do-over concept today to make your life a little less stressed? Leaders carry their own personal do-over tool that they use like an *Etch-a-Sketch* pad to quickly start over after making a mistake.

The vice president, still stinging from a mistake he just made, thought of the fore-runner of *Etch-a-Sketch* pad he had as a kid. He could still see that red wooden pencil that he used to draw thick black lines on that clean cellophane cover sheet. Over and over again. He'd work so diligently on a project. Then he would make a few mistakes. Get frustrated. Or bored. He would just want to start over. And instantly, he would get my wish. A clean slate. He just lifted that cellophane cover sheet off his drawing and his doodling disappeared. Oh how satisfying the sound of that cellophane sheet—sheeeeeeeeeer—erasing his drawing and nullifying his mistakes at the same time. And how rewarding to have another chance — a clean blank slate to challenge his imagination. Once again. Brand new.

These days, the vice president still has a more visible do-over drawing tool that helps him become a more strategic and creative thinker. He like to think of his do-over drawing tool as his personal Zamboni -- the ice resurfacing machine that glides across the rink between periods of a hockey game. That resurfacing machine clears away all the scratches, marks and rough spots that hard-charging, players etched into their ice-covered "cellphone" sheet of ice. That Zamboni machine also repairs and coats all the nicks and gashes in the ice to make it smoother and more efficient to skate on. These days whenever the vice president is frustrated in trying to solve a problem, he thinks of putting the Zamboni in his mind to work. He tries to clear away the clutter and often he recalls being a kid again with his cellophane covered drawing sheet and making that do-over sheeeeering sound like music to his ears.

Indeed the ability to clear your mind of previous information that could taint incoming new information is a key leadership skill. Consider the story of the college professor who visits the home of the Zen philosopher to learn more about the Buddhist belief of enlightenment through intuition and meditation. The Zen philosopher offered to pour the professor a cup of tea. He poured and poured —until the scalding hot tea cascaded over the brim of the cup, flooded the table and dripped onto the professor's lap. The enraged professor sprang to his feet and blurted to the Zen philosopher:

> *"You invite me into your home and then you pour hot tea all over me! The Zen philosopher calmly said: "You have come here to learn more about Zen. Your mind is like this cup. It is already filled with your own thoughts and opinions. To savor new ideas and new thoughts, you have to first empty your cup."*

These days, the vice president and other effective leaders try to empty their cups as often as they can so they can drink in new ideas. And maybe even stir them with that special red wooden pencil of yesteryear.

Today's ImproveMINT

Clear away the clutter in your mind on a regular basis to keep your leadership thinking in mint condition.

●

Well Begun = Half Done

Reading time: 4:41

Move 'em on, head 'em up.
Keep them doggies rollin'. Rawhide.

Those lyrics from the TV show *Rawhide* caught the attention of millions. And no wonder. Viewers were fascinated with how the real life cowboys of yesteryear could herd 3,000 cattle over a 1,000 mile route in two months, hoofing through 16 miles a day on average despite rain, terrain and pain. Amazing since most of us can't herd two cats into a room in a warm, comfortable home.

What's the secret? A quick start.

Over the first four days of the drive the cattle covered twice as many miles per day as they would average for the rest of the drive. The grueling accelerated effort paid off in fewer strays from homesick cattle too far from home to turn back at the slightest challenge.

That's why a quick start is an instructive leadership tactic for any complicated project filled with many moving parts. When you lead your next project think of this quick start as if it were a rocket thrust generating the escape velocity from a launching pad necessary to free the organization from the pull of gravity and the vice-like grip of the status quo. Yes, indeed well begun is half done as the Roman poet Horace observed in echoing Aristotle's notion that "beginning is said to be half the whole." And German philosopher Johann Wolfgang von Goethe noted: "Boldness has genius, power, and magic in it. Only engage and the mind grows heated, begin and the task will be completed." No wonder momentum-charged leaders tear a page out of author Joseph Heller's notebook. Heller says that after he has written the first sentence of a novel, he's "halfway home." No wonder momentum-charged leaders realize their capacity to act quickly is more powerful than their strength. Four-time Olympian Carl Lewis won nine gold medals in track and field for the United States. But he didn't win the 100 and 200 meter races in his last two Olympics (1992, 1996) after winning both races in his first two Olympics (1984, 1988). Poor starts hurt him even though after the start he was the fastest runner, according to James Gleick, author of *Faster, The Acceleration of Just About Everything.*

Well begun is half done.

Indeed, that's why the most influential leaders are so productive and powerful at the start of a project. They perform as if they were personal electrical generating plants. They know they HAVE TO generate enough (electrical) energy QUICKLY and POWERFULLY at the start (220,000 volts) to effectively meet the resistance in the wires over a long distance and still reach homes at 120 volts. That's why momentum-charged Presidents of the United States try to ride herd in their first 100 days in office. And that's why careers and projects get off the ground with as much FRONT END acceleration as do 747 jets burning three times as much fuel on takeoff as they do at cruising speed.

So go ahead, saddle up. And get a quick start on your own cattle drive of sorts. Accelerate to exhilarate like a leader. Make your mark from the start. *"Move 'em on, head 'em up. Keep them doggies rollin'. Rawhide. "*

Today's ImproveMINT

Accelerate quickly out of the blocks
to keep your leadership thinking in mint condition.

●

CREATIVITY

Leadership Mints
Extra Bonus

Give 'em the VIP Treatment

See the following pages 88-99 for an example of creative values-based leadership influencing greater employee discretionary behavior that fortifies the bottom line.

Give 'em
The VIP Treatment

Reading time: 22:56

Enthusiastically, the retail clerk raced into work and eagerly took charge of his cash register. He couldn't wait to start serving his customers with a personal banter that turned the tedious jobs of both the shopper and the cashier into a duet, a playful partnership of you-buy-I bag-and-we-smile together. He was good at what he did and everyone around him – his bosses, his peers, and his customers—knew it. Business was slow on this early Sunday morning. His cash register would remain silent at least for now. Neither his magic wand – the scanning device—nor his magnetic smile would be dazzling anyone right now.

With no customers in sight, he began sweeping and cleaning his cashier's station. But soon he got bored. He needed something more creative, more productive, and more meaningful to do. His manager knew just what to do to engage his star performer. He assigned him to serve as a greeter at the main entrance where the consummate people person would have a chance to interact with everyone who came into the store. But the twinkle in the eyes of the star performer faded again. He got bored. Again. After all, he was a roll-your-up-sleeves-and-get-busy type retail clerk. Finally the   boredom overwhelmed him. Frustrated, he reached into the large pocket of his store-issued vest and pulled out a small pocket-book that he read during breaks and lunch. "Ah, at last I have something to do," he said to himself, as he stood guard at the entrance while reading his book. His manager saw that red cover from a distance and like an enraged bull charged at the retail clerk from what seemed halfway across the store. "You can't be reading a book on the job like that!"

The stunned employee fired back with equal venom: "Yes I can!" Then he boomed even louder in an uncharacteristic bombastic tone. "Oh, yes I can!"

"No, no, no...." the manager retorted, walking away in utter disgust.

The manager was on the verge of firing an employee whose star had always burned brightly as an ideal employee. And now the star performer was on the verge of quitting or being fired. The flagrant book reader on company time was so defiant, the manager ordered him to get out of his sight: "Go face (straighten) the soup cans (on the shelf)." The seething employee bolted out of his greeter's role, eager to be doing something —anything— other than just standing around aimlessly and staring blankly into the isolation of the store on this raw morning.

The manager and the employee hardly spoke the rest of the day even as customer traffic increased and the cashier resumed his mastery over the scanning wand. But the magic was gone. The employee worked with less vim and vigor for the rest of the day. The flare-up hurt. The business lost the full services of a high-performing employee. The manager lost any rapport he had earned with the employee. And the star employee felt de-valued — as if his more than 14-months of previous stellar service counted for nothing. He felt humiliated, scorned and disrespected. He took his frustration out on the company's bottom-line with less productivity and little or no creative problem-solving. There has to be a better way of correcting the behavior of good employees who do bad things. Let's face it: reading a book while you are on the job, as a greeter of customers, isn't exactly staying customer focused. The star employee was definitely wrong. Could it be the manager was also wrong? What would a leader have done that the manager didn't?

How would a leader rein in the employee without raining on the employee's parade of previous high performance? A leader would have given the offending employee the V-I-P treatment where the offending employee is treated much more holistically than as just a Very Important Person. In this case, V-I-P is a three-step process that a leader "in mint condition" would use to turn an ordinary "Fire 'em" solution into an extraordinary "Fire 'em Up" resolution. Effective leaders think of V-I-P as a three-step process of Validating, Identifying, and Preserving engaged, creative and productive employees regardless of changing work environment conditions:

- **In Validating:**

    The Leader in Mint Condition FIRST acknowledges the star performer's reputation for productive and creative work.

- **In Identifying:**

    The Leader in Mint Condition assesses the situation and defines the CURRENT value of an employee's skill sets that have contributed to his or her reputation for productive behavior.

- **In Preserving:**

    The Leader in Mint Condition reminds the employee of his or her stellar reputation and provides him or her a face-saving way to preserve the integrity of that previous performance especially when the working conditions change (such as a slow day in the store) or conflict ensues.

Study the following VIP Treatment as it would be applied to the situation already referenced: A high performing employee is reading a book while serving as greeter at the door of a retail store. His team leader approaches the employee and says:

VALIDATING

"Joe, you always are highly productive and even now when it's slow you find a way to stay busy, reading. I think of you as the ultimate multi-tasker. I wonder though if you could be tarnishing your reputation for the way you always anticipate the needs of our customers if you aren't able to gain immediate eye contact as they enter the store.

IDENTIFYING

"I know it's boring standing here when few customers come through the door. But I like to think of myself as the captain of the ship when I have door duty. I am welcoming people on board this ship. And I am not sure my customers coming on board would think the best of me as their captain if I wasn't focused more on them than reading.

PRESERVING

"Joe you are the captain of this ship right now in your greeter's role and your passengers – your customers—need what you give them so creatively, so productively day in and day out at your register just as much here at the door: your undivided attention. You've always been a great example to the other employees as a top performer. It will get busier soon and then you will be going back to your cash register. But right now, Captain, we need you to read the eyes of our customers like you do so well and save the reading of those pages in that book for later."

Joe shoved the book back in his pocket and smiled proudly as the leader nodded, his demeanor sincere, his tone respectful, and his attitude thankful for having such a productive employee on his staff. Soon the store got busier and Joe returned to his first love – cashiering – with even more energy and enthusiasm. And even more magic in his wand. He had been validated. His work identified. And his reputation preserved. Joe had been given the VIP Treatment by a leader who sought to care by design rather than from a manager who sought to control by default. Indeed leaders who provide the VIP treatment—of Validating, Identifying and Preserving—often find their staffs respond with considerable discretionary creative energy, spirit and drive on the job, according to research on employee engagement and job satisfaction.

Maybe that's why Henry Ford said, "You can take my factories, burn up my buildings but give me my PEOPLE and I'll build the business right back." Notice that Henry Ford did not say "Give me my employees." Indeed, his PEOPLE were much more than employees. His PEOPLE were the heartbeat of the company-- the spirit, energy and drive behind his company. Without a focus on people beyond a strong back and a pair of hands, a would-be leader can fall victim to a costly bidding war to retain a talented and committed workforce. However the most effective leaders know the way to compensate their "people" without going broke: They pay employees more than money. The most effective leaders pay their people respect. In fact, General Dwight Eisenhower paid respect to the common soldier. "In our army, every private had at least a second lieutenant's gold bars somewhere in him and he was helped and encouraged to earn them." Napoleon also paid respect to a common soldier who delivered a message just as the soldier's horse dropped dead from exhaustion. "Here take my horse," Napoleon said. The soldier balked. "Your horse is too good for me, a common soldier." Napoleon scoffed: "Nothing is too good or too magnificent for a common soldier." Napoleon knew that paying another respect can be more enriching than money. In fact paying another respect can save money. Take it from the new County Sheriff in Ohio who saved 80 percent in vandalism costs over the previous year in part by paying respect to some of the incarcerated. The Sheriff awarded more perks to inmates who were charged with lesser crimes. He treated them with respect. He gave them the VIP Treatment:

- He **validated** them as upstanding citizens who happened to make a mistake.
- He *identified* them as being law-abiding responsible adults for the most part.
- And he ***preserved*** their sense of personal responsibility and confidence while in jail.

The VIP-treating Sheriff gave one bald prisoner a baseball cap to help him keep warm. He allowed another to work part time in the county's garage. And the new VIP-treating Sheriff gave others regular smoking breaks. The net result? Vandalism by disgruntled prisoners decreased so much that maintenance costs that year were only 20 percent of the previous year. Nurturing leaders are the key. As David Kelley, the founder of IDEO the leading industrial design firm says "If we were to measure what makes a leader here it would be to measure how nurturing people are." Indeed VIP nurturing leaders know the power in treating others the way you would want to be treated. VIP nurturing leaders embrace the leadership sentiments of Confucius who said: "If you use laws to direct people and punishments to control them, they will only evade the laws and develop no conscience. But if you guide them by virtue and control them by customs, they will have a conscience and a sense of what is right." Then in knowing what's right, in feeling empowered, in getting the VIP Treatment, your people will feel so VALIDATED, so IDENTIFIED, so PRESERVED (think Pre-Served) that they will perform with a creative burst of discretionary behavior that can consistently exceed the expectations of the leaders they report to and the customers they serve.

Beware of InterFEARance

In leading others faithfully with the VIP Treatment, the most effective leaders eradicate the barriers and obstacles – anything that smacks of interFEARence in the apt observation of author Alan Fine in his book *You Already Know How To Be Great*. Replacing that interFEARence with a partnership of CONFIDEnce where you confide in others and leverage the VIP Treatment between leaders and team members that stimulates significant and sustained discretionary performance from employees and bolsters bottom-line results.

For example consider Steelcase Inc., a company founded more than 100 years ago (1912 in Grand Rapids, Michigan) that has consistently led the office furniture industry in worldwide sales. The company's well-developed VIP Treatment of —Validating, Identifying and Preserving the dignity and worth of each individual employee —has unleashed extraordinary discretionary performance even in what most others would call the most ordinary and even the most routine— even boring— jobs: working as a waitress, a truck driver and a janitor. Mary was a server in the guest dining room at Steelcase Inc.'s corporate headquarters. That day she set the luncheon table with the finest china, the shiniest silverware, the sparkling crystal glasses —and a corroding carburetor, a bent fender and other assorted aging motorcycle parts of days gone by. A 10-foot-wide banner hung on a wall: *Harley-Davidson, More than a Machine.* Mary was there to serve the executives from the famous motorcycle manufacturer more than just food. The professional waitress also served them a few of her own fond memories in Hog Heaven riding Harleys. She smiled at the memory of riding on the back of her brother's Harley to high school so many years ago. Her eyes glistened as she scanned the carburetor and the fender from a friend's Harley that she had displayed in the dining room like so many artifacts from a unique and rewarding culture. Mary felt that her employer—Steelcase—had VALIDATED her self-worth, IDENTIFIED her values, and that PRESERVED her personal integrity that she served her customers above and   beyond the service levels indicated in her   job description.

Likewise, Paul gleamed and beamed with the VIP Treatment he experienced as a truck driver at Steelcase. Paul found his vocal cords vibrating whenever he saw a Steelcase 18-wheeler on the open road. Guitar in hand and a song in his heart, Paul found himself writing a love song of sorts to the Steelcase truck fleet. He inspired eight other Steelcase drivers to join him in recording the song— *Blue & Chrome* — that celebrated the pride and discipline of driving Steelcase trucks.

Meanwhile, Craig, the Steelcase janitor pushed more than a broom. Steelcase gave him the VIP treatment as a talented artist who volunteered to paint on his own time colorful murals that brightened the walls in a manufacturing plant. He painted a 12-foot wide, 8-foot high seascape mural that featured a bright orange sun spraying its orange and yellow hues across the seagull-filled blue sky. Craig felt he had been Validated, Identified and Preserved with the VIP Treatment. When you feel that Valued, that Identified, that Preserved you are more likely to want to get to work on time where you are appreciated for who you are as much as for what you do. Maybe that's why Diligent Dick had perfect attendance for 41 years as a production worker at Steelcase. Not even a bloody hand injury and 18 stitches OFF the job could keep Diligent Dick from showing up to work on time just 10 hours later. So what if 17-inches of snow fell in one 30-hour period? Diligent Dick would get up at 2:30 am to shovel his driveway and still get to work on time by 5:30 am. He felt a personal connection to his bosses and peers at Steelcase where leaders focus as much on their EQ (Emotional Quotient) as their IQ (intelligence Quotient). Maybe that's why Bob Pew, the CEO and Chairman of Steelcase from the mid-1950s to the early 1990s, said: "Business is a social entity and as such it becomes a human experience."

WE CARE

In fact, business is regarded as such a human experience at Luck Companies in Richmond, VA that the company founder would cook lunch for his then 14 employees every day at the worksite in the late 1920s and early 1930s. Charles Luck Jr. purchased an old railroad dining car and had it situated near the quarry where his modern-day Fred Flintstones carved out rocks and crushed stone, sand and gravel in helping Luck Companies today become one of the nation's largest family-owned construction aggregate companies. The hands-on cooking by the company founder served as a symbol for a promise he made to his employees before and during the Great Depression: they would be the first to be paid in tough economic times. He kept his promise. Do right by your employees and they will do right by the company, he proclaimed shortly after founding the company in 1923.

The founder's son fostered that same pay-it-forward, caring and sharing philosophy when he became the Chief Executive Officer. He even placed signage in key areas throughout the company proclaiming "We Care." That caring culture anchored a quality driven loyal workforce that has sparked significant growth over more than 90 years. However the company grew too fast in the late 1990s, quadrupling its employees from 300 to nearly 1300 by 2005. The growth overwhelmed the company when its management structure decentralized and destabilized the very foundation of its culture. Executives began aggressively competing with each other for resources to manage the company's growth. New hires exacerbated the contentious business climate while snarky executives rattled their sabers in a plethora of meetings-after-the-meeting. Backstabbing ensued. And an air of corporate dysfunction engulfed the company. "We had lost our way," admitted Mark Fernandes, the Chief Leadership Officer at Luck Companies.

Then in 2003, the grandson of the founder and current Chief Executive Officer Charles Luck IV launched a Values-Based Leadership initiative to align all of its employees around key values and beliefs that drive the mission of the company to "ignite human potential through Values Based Leadership and positively impacting the lives of others around the world." The company reinforced its roots of caring for employees and the employees responded by caring even more about the company and its customers.

Today, Luck Companies continues to outpace its competition, doubling its direct cash generated per employee from 2006-2013 while developing all of the current 850 employees at all levels as leaders. "One of our core beliefs is that all people are born with extraordinary potential to make a positive difference," observed current CEO, Charles Luck IV. That's why Luck Companies has invested over a decade in executing its own version of the VIP Treatment-- of Validating, Identifying and Preserving --- "who we are and what we believe" says Fernandes. But not all executives could dance to the changing music. They wouldn't adapt to the new corporate rhythms. They couldn't get in tune with the new corporate vibrations of doing well by doing good and they were asked to find another dance floor. The new Values-Based Leading Luck

Companies needed leaders who could move in step WITH others not step OVER others. Luck Companies started its new dance lessons at the top of the organization with the CEO and vice presidents of the company willing to step up and work through "who they really are on the inside, how they show up on the outside (personality style and behaviors) and what impact they are having on others around them," Fernandes said. A former stone mason, Fernandes describes himself as a "recovering jerk" who initially struggled in becoming the Values-Based Leader that he is today. "I had to learn to look in the mirror not out of the windshield and man that is hard," Fernandes recalled. He faced that challenge and now is one of the nation's few corporate vice presidents (non CEO or president) who has the formal title of Chief Leadership Officer and actively shares his company's Values-Based-Leadership principles both inside and outside the company. His leadership efforts have paid off.

Today his company's workforce consistently scores virtually twice the average in job satisfaction surveys (97% surveyed, 88% engaged 86% enabled 81% effectiveness). Mike is one of those employees at Luck Companies who feels so engaged on the job and so enabled to do his job that he performs above and beyond his job description. He delivers sand to construction sites. In the winter he regularly goes the extra yard for his customers, helping them save time thawing the sand on cold winter mornings. Mike voluntarily sets up a fire barrel and kindling the night before so his customers will be able to more efficiently thaw the frozen sand so they can more quickly start their construction work day as masons. The fire barrel set-up is not in his job description but it is part and parcel of the way he does his job. He treats his customers the same way the company treats him —with the VIP Treatment --of Validating, Identifying and Preserving their needs and values.

That sense of caring did not come easy for all employees at Luck Companies, especially when the company first launched its Values-Based Leadership initiatives. Executives even debated the extent they had to care about others. But then the vision of the current CEO focused his company's mission to do more than merely keep the cash flowing. Charles Luck IV's broadened his company's mission to ignite the potential in others. He led the company through a serious investment in training and development. The flagship leadership program at Luck Companies extends over a year and includes 10 days in the classroom of coaching, service projects and 360 feedback assessments. The company's officers and top 40 leaders worked on their own personal values and then taught others throughout the company. They not only learned to care for others but also to care about getting feedback from others above them and below them on the organizational chart.

They studied situational leadership styles. They took personality tests. They learned to champion collaboration and teamwork. They learned to work with a greater sense of personal awareness and emotional intelligence that influenced others. And most importantly they learned how to seek and be open to meaningful and constructive feedback. Today Luck Companies fosters a robust, feedback-oriented culture where diversity is championed and decision-making shared so broadly that rank and file employees readily accept greater responsibility within the privately-held company.

For example, the plant manager tasked a 14-person maintenance team to assume the primary role in hiring a mechanic. The plant manager **validated** the judgment of his entire maintenance team, **identified** their trustworthiness and **preserved** their loyalty in giving them the VIP treatment to conduct the hiring process that would have been previously conducted by the plant manager. Dan, the newly hired mechanic, got a first-hand look at how leaders care for their employees and how their employees care for their leaders. *We Care* isn't just a slogan at Luck Companies. It's THE WAY of doing business as a values-based leader unlocking the potential in all employees to better serve their customers. With the VIP Treatment.

COLLABORATING
Part II

"In every office you hear

the threads of love and joy

and fear and guilt, the cries for

celebration and reassurance.

"And somehow you know

connecting those threads

is what you are supposed to do.

And business takes care of itself."

-Jim Autry, Author,
Love and Profit--
The Art of Caring Leadership

Mint 35

Leaders Are
Great Kissers

Reading time: 3:23

Pucker up. How good a kisser are you? Your kissing behavior could be a measure of your leadership capability. No way you say. Well consider the following description of an optimal kiss in this excerpt from Robert A. Heinlein's novel: *Stranger in a Strange Land:*

"Anne tell me something. What's so special about the way Michael kisses?" Anne looked dreamy and then dimpled. "Michael gives a kiss his whole attention. Oh, rats! I do too." Anne shook her head. "No, some men try to. Men who did a very good job of it indeed have kissed me.

"But they don't really give kissing a woman their whole attention. They can't. No matter how hard they try, some parts of their minds are on something else: Missing the last bus. Their own techniques in kissing. Worry about their jobs. Or money. Or something. Now Michael doesn't have any technique. But when he kisses you he isn't doing anything else. Not anything. You're his whole universe for that moment. And the moment is eternal because he doesn't have any plans and he isn't going anywhere. Just kissing you." She shivered. "A woman notices. It's overwhelming."

Leaders are great kissers. They kiss you with something more overwhelming, more engaging and more exciting than their lips. They kiss you with their eyes. They kiss you with their ears. They kiss you with a magnetic smile that bathes you in a feeling of fidelity and security, a feeling of warmth and understanding, a feeling of complete acceptance and validation. And they kiss you with a feeling of respect, of high regard.

Indeed when you regard someone or something, the dictionary says you show "respect or consideration." You take a "protective interest." You "estimate the worth of something or someone." You might recall that scene in the movie *Babe* when the sheep rancher first visually kisses the pig--Babe. The narrator says that the rancher and the pig did more than just eye each other. "They regarded each other." Leaders in particular regard their staffs.

- As Great Kissers, leaders make each staff member feel that he or she is needed, and loved for who they are without any reservation.
- As Great Kissers, leaders can turn a routine encounter into a memorable experience.

Consider the post office customer who wanted to send a package first class. The post office clerk looked into the eyes of the customer--carefully regarding him--- and then planted a verbal kiss on his lips: "I'll mark it first class right here before your eyes," she said. That leader made her customer feel a sense of recognition and appreciation. That leader made her customer feel special. Someone has acknowledge him, someone truly listened to him. Intently. And as a leader she regarded him without any reservation. That's what leaders do. Even in routine transactions, the most effective leaders don't kiss you OFF. They turn you ON. Professionally. Intentionally. And meaningfully. With a proverbial kiss.

Today's ImproveMINT

Concentrate fully to keep
your leadership thinking in mint condition.

●

Mint 36

Leaders Are
Great Lovers

Reading time: 3:51

General Norman Schwarzkopf surprised a lot of battle-worn military leaders when he said to his colleagues: "I shall always love you. I will never, ever, ever forget you." No that isn't a line out of a sexy movie or an excerpt from a sensational tabloid. Significantly, those words gushed from the heart of a General in the United States Army during a public speech he delivered in front of his fellow military leaders and a national television audience. The General pledged that he would always love and never forget his soldiers that he had led to victory in the Persian Gulf War in 1991. Schwarzkopf was retiring from the army after 31 years. But he could never retire from his soldiers. He knew that effective leaders are lovers. Forever.

The most effective leaders love and respect their colleagues and followers and consequently bring out the best in them. General Dwight Eisenhower worked at developing his love for the troops. In the four months before D-Day, the leader of the Allied Forces visited troops in 26 divisions at 24 air fields and on five warships. His love brought out the best in those soldiers who would heroically invade Normandy Beach and lead the United States and its allies ultimately to win World War II. The lover in the leader needed to express up close his appreciation for — and love of — the soldier on the front lines. So passionately. So poignantly. So personally. Eisenhower used those visits with the troops to refresh himself as much as boost the morale of the troops. Eisenhower said: "Whenever I became fed up with meetings, paperwork and protocol, I could rehabilitate myself by a visit with the troops among them talking to each other as individuals and listening to each other's stories I was refreshed and could return to headquarters reassured that hidden behind administrative entanglements the military was an enterprise manned by human beings."

Human beings.

Leaders never lose focus on who follows them. Human beings. Not troops. Not employees. Not voters. Not stockholders. Not what they do for a living but who they are at living. People. People with feelings. People with dreams, ambitions and concerns. People are uppermost in the most effective leader's decision making. With a focus on people, leaders love 'em and their people love them back. Take it from former president and chief executive officer of SAS, Scandinavian Airlines Jan Carlzon who says: "You have to manage by love; you have to create an atmosphere in which people feel they are respected, that you have faith in them, even that you love them. They will dare to take risks. Dare to use their imagination." And become even more successful than they thought they could be.

Take it from Reggie Jackson, the prolific home run hitter of Mr. October fame who batted his way into the Baseball Hall of Fame over 21 years with the New York Yankees and Oakland A's. "A great manager has a knack for making ballplayers think they are better than they think they are," Jackson said. "He forces you to have a good opinion of yourself. He lets you know he believes in you. He makes you get more out of yourself. And once you learn how good you really are, you never settle for playing anything less than your very best." Leaders bring out the best in others. With love.

Today's ImproveMINT

Love and respect your staff /teammates
to keep your leadership thinking in mint condition.

●

Goosing
The Goose Bumps

Reading time: 3:45

After four years of marriage, Debbie was thrilled that at last she might be pregnant. She was so excited when she stepped into the examination room at her doctor's office. After the exam, her doctor seemed to forget that she was still in the room. He looked over to the attending nurse and reported in a clinical drone: "The cervix is blue. That indicates pregnancy." The obstetrician made a feint attempt at eye contact with his patient. Then he brusquely left the examination room and hurried off to his next patient. Debbie felt abandoned on her first trip to Mommy Land. She expected at least a warm inviting smile but she got only a cold dismissive shoulder. No way. No how. She fumed.

A few days later Debbie saw another doctor. He conducted a similar examination with similar   results but with a decidedly different response. The doctor shook Debbie's   hand   and   beamed: "Congratulations, congratulations, you are going to have a baby!" Debbie beamed. She felt goose bumps running down her back. She was so elated. So thrilled. So fulfilled.

Goosing the goose bumps — triggering a sense of well-being in others—is a critical skill for the most effective leaders. When feelings more than just the facts are shared, trust soars and mutual understanding and confidence ensues in any relationship, particularly one as intimate as doctor/patient. With feelings comes a human bond that cements conviction and leads to outstanding service, quality and performance. In fact, feelings impact the bottom line. Doctors are sued less often if they demonstrate more of a listening/caring/feeling posture in their initial meeting with the patient, research shows. And with that caring treatment, the patient is more likely to respond favorably to their medical treatment. As Voltaire noted: "The art of medicine consists of amusing the patient while nature cures the disease." As a leader how are you "amusing" your followers, how are you goosing their goose bumps to gain greater results? Goose the goose bumps —the feelings — in your people and you leverage your bottom line, according to Jim Autry, a former chief executive officer of a multi-million company. The author of *Love and Profit*, Autry writes: ***"In every office you hear the threads of love and joy and fear and guilt, the cries for celebration and reassurance. And somehow you know connecting those threads is what you are supposed to do. And business takes care of itself."***

How do you connect those threads? With emotional intelligence. With a high degree of paying attention to how you feel and paying even more attention to how others around you feel particularly under stress, according to Daniel Goleman, author of *Emotional Intelligence*. He calls emotional intelligence the "sine qua non of leadership." Indeed without emotional intelligence, without feelings, there can be no leadership. That's because it is "feelings that set a man thinking and not thought that sets him feeling," observed author George Bernard Shaw. Feelings count. That's why author Tom Peters says, "leadership is 100 percent about emotion." That's why The Center for Creative Leadership found that "insensitivity to others" is the most cited reason that leaders fail. And that's why poet Maya Angelou observed: "People will forget what you said. People will forget what you did. But people will always remember how you made them feel." Leaders goose the goose bumps.

Today's ImproveMINT

Express your feelings
to keep your leadership thinking in mint condition.

R-E-S-P-E-C-T
Putting the Spell on Others
Reading time: 3:33

Belligerent, the fuming teenager couldn't contain himself any longer: "You bitch!" he erupted, firing his eyes with just as much vile as his words toward a veteran officer at the Juvenile Detention Center. Darlene, poised and confident, paused. She looked deep into the glowering eyes of her verbal attacker, his pulsating veins dancing frantically in his neck.

"Now just a minute," Darlene shot back, firing her words like bullets between the eyes of the teenager. "Have I ever called you anything but your given name? Have I ever shown you any disrespect for who you are as a person? What gives you the right to call me anything but my given name?" The teenager lowered his eyes and lowered his voice. "Yeah, yeah," he grumbled and mumbled more to himself than anyone else. The anger-filled veins in his neck slowed their dance from reggae to a ballet. "Yeah, yeah," he repeated. Darlene's eyes beamed a warm glow on him that he felt more than he saw from the Juvenile Detention Center officer.

The teenager walked out of that gymnasium at the detention center, leaving behind much more than his anger. He felt different. More confident. Less arrogant. More disciplined. Less defiant. After all, the teenager couldn't remember when anyone told him they would never disrespect him as a person. Suddenly Aretha Franklin's voice popped into his head. She is singing "R-E-S-P-E-C-T" echoing the Juvenile Detention Center officer's admonition that respect begets respect. Darlene demonstrated a key leadership skill: Love the sinner; hate the sin. Darlene could have reacted to the teenager with her own passionate barrage of verbal abuse or authoritarian measures. Darlene could have taken charge of that situation. But loving leaders do not have to TAKE charge. They are always IN CHARGE of themselves. They are always IN CHARGE of treating others with dignity and respect and influencing others to behave productively. And as a leader, Darlene has found the more she respects them, the better they respect her over time. In fact research at the University of Kansas reaffirms Darlene's leadership effectiveness. In that study, mothers kept track of how often they paid attention to their problem children's good behavior. As the mothers became more supportive the children's behaviors improved.

Leaders see more than meets the eye. They see beneath that rock-solid exterior that some hide behind. They see the faces of integrity invariably beaming through the hardened and sullied rock much like the sculptor saw the 60-foot tall faces of George Washington, Abraham Lincoln, Thomas Jefferson and Teddy Roosevelt long before he took the first chisel to Mount Rushmore. Sculptor Gutzon Borglum said he removed unwanted rock and brought out the best of what was already there. He echoed the sentiments of Michelangelo who said before creating his *David* that "the shape is already in the stone."

Likewise, Darlene reinforced the leadership tenet that everyone has value even its hidden deep below the surface, clouded in circumstance or buried in bigotry. As Andrew Carnegie once said: "You develop people in the same way you mine for gold. In the gold mine you move tons of dirt to find an ounce of gold. You don't look for the dirt. You look for the gold." Even if someone first calls you a "bitch."

Today's ImproveMINT

Respect all, even those who disrespect you
to keep your leadership thinking in mint condition.

●

Mint 39

Exercising Your Navel Intelligence

Reading time: 3:39

G o ahead. No one's looking. Touch your belly button. You now have your finger on the most critical button you can push to engage your sense of leadership. After all, your belly button marks the spot where your umbilical cord nourished you to life. So too your employees, customers and vendors nourish and sustain your organization today through a similar mutually-dependent connection. You need them and they need you.

That's why the most effective leaders leverage their "navel" intelligence with a focus on making sure all parts of the interdependent organization stay connected and nourished. Your belly button is a visual reminder to all leaders of the enormous growth potential in staying connected — considering a baby in the womb grows over a million times in weight and 240 times in length! With that kind of stunning growth, your belly button reminds us that no one is an island, that we all need each other. "People who need people are the luckiest people in the world," sings Barbra Streisand.

If so, then some of those luckiest people in the 1960s lived in Roseto, a small town in Pennsylvania. They were well-connected and very healthy. Their close family ties were cited for the low incidents of heart disease, even though Roseto residents had a high fat diet and did not exercise. But then, when people in the town drifted apart from each other —when they became disconnected, when they cut their proverbial umbilical cords— their incidence of heart attacks increased. The evidence shows your health is less at risk when you stay connected. Strengthening your connections to family and friends can even stave off Death from knocking on your door—at least for a while. Consider these two deadly disconnects:

- A Yale University study showed that heart patients with no emotional support (friends and family) were more than twice as likely to die within a month after discharge from the hospital.
- A University of Michigan study found that men who lack social networks (connections) of family, friends, or church groups experience death rates 1-3 times higher.

The human need to stay connected to other human beings is so strong that a Vietnam POW said he would endure torture rather than give up his attempts to maintain communication with other POWs. "Man can stand more pain if he is linked with others in communications," writes Captain Eugene "Red" McDaniel in his book *Scars and Stripes.*

In their drive to make those connections, leaders feed—and feed off of —others in much the same way a room with pendulum clocks set at a different swing rates will synchronized without any manual or electronic intervention. That's why staying connected can turn a dangerous situation around. Consider this example from the world of chemistry. Chlorine can be caustic by itself and in high concentration dangerous. But if you combine chlorine with sodium the resulting compound is something you enjoy on popcorn and hundreds of other foods—table salt. Make a connection. Leverage your navel intelligence. Get in touch. With your belly button.

Today's ImproveMINT

Stay connected to others
to keep your leadership thinking in mint condition.

●

Mint 40

Playing Your ACE
In a Stacked Deck

Reading time: 3:25

Her idea was sound. The highly-recommended, newly-hired vice president checked her facts. She had the documentation. She presented her idea clearly and concisely. No one could refute the thinking process or the expected results. The idea had already worked elsewhere. It could work here. It should work here. It will work here, she assured anyone and everyone. Yet most of the decision-makers in the company she needed to persuade remained poker faced even though they saw that indeed the company could benefit from her idea. But her idea never got off the ground, even though she had done the proper research, even though she had earned third-party endorsement from her peers outside the company.

What happened? Why didn't her idea fly? Perhaps this highly credentialed and experienced would-be leader forgot to first EARN THE RIGHT to be in the right. And that means sharing much more than what you know in your head. It's knowing in your heart what others need to know FIRST about you. Too many would-be leaders learn too late that before you can share your ideas —your competency—with decision makers, you first have to establish your compatibility with them and with their leadership principles. You first have to share your allegiance to their values or be saddled as a Rebel Without a Pause. And experience shows time and again Rebels Without a Pause in an organization can threaten more than enlighten. However those who first pause to think more about their audience can become persuasive leaders. In pausing first and focusing on their audience of decision makers, they figure out how to FIRST wrap their new idea around an existing idea or concept already adopted throughout the organization. Rebels With a Pause quickly learn how to pause for the cause and play their ACE. They learn how to stack the deck to get their ideas heard, understood, accepted and acted upon. ACE is a 3-step persuasion process of *Acknowledging* the current leadership culture, earning *Compatibility* with decision makers and *Extending* an accepted value or belief to incorporate your proposal. Newly–minted leaders in particular and all leaders in general play that ACE of persuasion especially when the deck of familiarity is stacked against them. Play your ACE like this:

Acknowledging

Acknowledge the expertise around you. Focus on the positives of tradition. Credit the success of the past. Credit your boss. Share the limelight with others.

Compatibility

Establish your compatibility with executive decision-makers regarding the company's values, mission and vision. Then cement your credibility. Seek mutual allies (solicit sponsors within the company in advance) to link your new idea to a proven principle recognized for many years within the company.

Extending

Present your idea as an extension of the values and vision of the company. Show how your new idea follows on that same train of thought the other decision makers are already riding. Gain trust. Earn the right to be right. And ACE your place as a leader.

Today's ImproveMINT

Seek compatibility first in persuading others
to keep your leadership thinking in mint condition.

●

Mint 41

Becoming Chairman
Of the Bored

Reading time: 3:21

Bored, the injured employee on a restricted work assignment complained to the company president that he needed something more challenging than "busy work" during his recovery. The president, valuing the enthusiasm and loyalty of the production worker, responded: "From now on you are reporting to me. You are in charge of preparing our showroom for customer visits." The injured employee was no longer bored. He was burning with a passion of purpose. The president exercised his role as Chairman of the Bored, a critical role of aligning the organization's talent and resources.

Now the injured employee was designated a bona-fide member of the customer visit team and therefore in regular contact with the sales department. The employee said he felt like he was "really part of the company again." The company president acted like a leader in designating autonomy, saying "You're in charge." He did not simply delegate responsibility ("Go see the personnel department for another job assignment.") The most effective leaders are more apt to designate than just delegate.

- When you DESIGNate, you empower others to DESIGN their own working process.
- When you DESIGNate, you yield plenty of personal latitude to DESIGN your creative output. Consider the Designated Hitter in baseball. The DH is put in charge of getting hits in whatever creative fashion he chooses.

However, when you deleGATE, you provide employees a more limited access through the gate of your power— a gate of a predetermined scope of operations and expectations. DeleGATED employees are like puppets on a string: their ability to perform depends on so many (purse) strings attached.

- When you deleGATE with plenty of strings attached, you can breed a complacency that robs a person of his or her spirit, energy and drive for their work.
- When you deleGATE with plenty of strings attached, you breed a complacency that starves the soul of ecstasy and excitement, that starves the soul of recognition and reward, and that starves the soul of the feeling of making a commitment and achieving a goal.
- When you deleGATE with plenty of strings attached, you breed a complacency that strangles initiative and enterprise with its web of apathy and indifference.

But when you exercise your role as Chairman of the Bored, you curb complacency and unleash creativity.

You DESIGNate. You don't simply deleGATE.

You anoint for all time more than appoint for a specific time. And in the process you turn your bored employees into boring employees —boring deep into the customer-rich centers of your company to hit pay dirt. With the passion of purpose, a passion that *Gooses the Goose Bumps* (See page 105, Mint 37) and provides a *Heart Transplant of Another Kind* (See page 115, Mint 42).

Today's ImproveMINT

DESIGNate more than deleGATE
to keep your leadership thinking in mint condition.

●

Heart Transplant
Of Another Kind

Reading time: 3:45

Methodically, the clerk in the grocery store's deli counter seized a stack of smoked turkey displayed in the glass case. She placed her catch on the scale. The blue digital numbers flashed 1.01 pounds. The customer was impressed with the precision the clerk demonstrated in selecting the exact amount of turkey. "Your accuracy must come from years of experience," the customer said. Sharon smiled and her eyes beamed. "No, not really. I 'm just helping out here today. I work most of the time as a cashier in the store but I guess my heart is really in deli."

It's 9 a.m. on Monday morning. Do you know where your staff's hearts are? The most effective leaders do. They and their staffs are aligned to best accomplish the mission. Body and mind, hearts and souls are in the right place at the right time. Fully aligned. As a leader, you know your role is to orchestrate the best individual performance you can out of each of your people. As a leader you know your role is to insure that your employees get a chance to sing their song --to express their music with their optimum instrument -on their optimum stage.

Yet sometimes leaders and their followers die with their music inside of them. Some may have been transferred out of a job they loved in the spirit of cross training and their music inside them died. Some may have been promoted to a job they gradually came to hate and their music inside them died. Others like Sharon may find a way to continually tune up the music inside them periodically if not strategically to turn up the volume on the music inside them. That's why the most effective leaders are skilled in performing heart transplants of another kind, aligning the jobs and workers, aligning skills and talents, aligning passions and purpose. Stretch assignments on paper can add value to an employee and the organization. But sometimes in reality those stretch assignments backfire on the organization and eventually on the employee if not properly vetted in advance and adequately monitored in progress.

Quality driven employees perform best when they are doing what they enjoy; when they are getting better at it every day and when they are in a pattern of yearning to learn and learning to earn. Learning expands performance on the job which extends learning on the job. The employee benefits in personal growth and the company benefits in added productivity. Leaders have to balance those individual and corporate needs very carefully or risk quality production. That's why the most effective leaders stay focused on their people's talents, passions and dreams in helping them chart their course through the organization's bottom line. They place their top people in roles to achieve their personal goals and give them plenty of support and a say where they feel they will be most productive to the company.

The lesson is clear for all effective leaders:

- Keep doling out action learning stretch assignments that infuse the employee with a sense of passion and purpose.
- Keep evaluating leaders, learners and situations.

But if the body rejects the new implant, be ready to perform a heart transplant of another kind. And add even more life to the organization.

Today's ImproveMINT

Align your staff's talents and skills
to keep your leadership thinking in mint condition.

●

Mint 43

Feeding FRIEND-zy
Reading time: 2:58

Neighboring cities shared the same contaminated water source, according to a legend. All of the residents in both cities fell victim to a disease that stiffened their elbows. They could move their arms but could not bend their elbows. All of the people in one of the towns starved to death. Yet most of the people in the other town —though still paralyzed —survived. How?

They fed each other.

Leaders feed others first in a kind of feeding "friend-zy" that nourishes and fosters mutual growth. They create a shared environment where their staffs feed off one another not feed on each other. They turn their companies into communities where citizens (i.e. employees) have a shared value, a common fate, a similar understanding. And that spirit of associating together is clearly reflected in more productive behaviors in much the same way horses are easier to handle if they are able to touch noses with other horses. Leaders recognize that they are like molecules of chloride: they exist only when they are paired, when they come together. Chemists tell us that chloride is too unstable to chemically exist on its own in nature. Chloride exists only when two molecules bond together in a liaison, which is French for "bond."

That kind of bonding is the crux of stellar teams in the world of sports, according to Phil Jackson, 11-time National Basketball Association champion coach. Writing in his book *Sacred Hoops,* Jackson sees the bonds that players develop on a team as embracing "a vision in which the group imperative takes precedence over individual glory and success comes from being awake, aware and in tune with others." The more IN TUNE you are with others the more

TUNED UP your personal engine is in revving your creative energy as author Peter Senge notes. That's why the most effective leaders realize that you only need one eye to see. But with two eyes you have better depth perception. Your eyes working as a team help you to add insight to your sight. Likewise, your insight on the factory floor or in a corporate department develops much like your balanced eye sight. The individual and the team are made for and by each other where "the strength of the pack is the wolf and the strength of the wolf is the pack," as poet Rudyard Kipling observed. A team is a group of people who need each other in order to accomplish their work. A team operates "as if it has a single heart beat," noted legendary University of Alabama college football coach Bear Bryant. No wonder. After all one CEO of a billion-dollar manufacturing company defines a company as a group of people who can be depended upon. The CEO notes the efficacy in teamwork: "When we turn our sights to each other and draw strength from each other, it is amazing what we can accomplish." Maybe that's why participating on a well-led team is so coveted, so valued and so predictive of a leader's performance, potential and promise. Take it from note author Peter Senge, writing in The Fifth Discipline: "When you ask people about what it's like being part of a great team, what's most striking is the meaningfulness of the experience. People talk about being part of something larger than themselves, of being connected, of being generative."

And maybe when you're on a well-led team, you're even able to fly like an angel. At least that's how Luciano de Crescenzo, the Italian actor and writer, assesses the spirit of collaboration: "We are each of us angels with only one wing and we can fly only by embracing one another." In a feeding "friend-zy!"

Today's ImproveMINT

Embrace your staff as part of your physical being
to keep your leadership thinking in mint condition.

Mint 44

Declaring Your Interdependence

Reading time: 3:21

G eese flying together honk at each other to keep themselves in a more efficient formation. They spell each other when the front-flier tires. The leader relies on the followers to honk encouragement to the leader to keep fighting the headwind. The followers do all the talking (honking) to cheer on their leader of the moment. Intermittently, the follower becomes the leader. And interdependently, the leader becomes the follower. Honker becomes honkee and the beat goes on. The most effective leaders not only stay in touch with their followers but intermittently climb down from the lofty ivory tower to see the world as their followers see it. And intermittently these most effective leaders even fly in formation ALONGSIDE their followers. The flying geese seem like parts of a well-oiled machine RELYING on each other for their own personal well-being let alone the productivity of the team.

Flying in formation and relying on each other, the geese teach us that leaders do their jobs better trusting and investing in others. Flying in formation and relying on each other, the geese teach us that leadership is a job not a position, as Max De Pree, the former Fortune 500 company CEO, writes in his book *Leadership Jazz.* And your staff "are not your people; you are theirs." Flying in formation and relying on each other, individual geese take turns as the leader. Researchers say geese can fly 71 percent farther in formation. The geese demonstrate they can fly farther with less effort. Researchers surmise the geese can feel it in their connection to —and focus on each other. Together— interdependently—leaders and followers bring out the best in each other: Together—interdependently—leaders and followers expand synergy more than simply expend energy. Leaders, in step with that dynamic dance of interdependence, know that it takes two to tango.   After all, every bell has its clapper, every bow its arrow and every pen its ink. Together— interdependently—leaders and followers rely on each other to become more professionally engaged, more creatively enriched and more personally satisfied as poet Mary Carolyn Davis observes in: *This is Friendship:*

> *"I love you,*
> *not only for what you are,*
> *but for what I am with you.*
> *"I love you*
> *not for what*
> *you have made of yourself,*
> *but for what*
> *you are making of me."*

Okay, maybe love is too strong a word for the relationship between the leader and his or her followers. Or is it? (See Mint 36 on page 103.) At any rate, that sense of interdependence makes for a long-lasting and fruitful relationship. As William James noted the symbiotic value of a leader and his or her followers: "The community stagnates with the impulse of the individual. And the impulse dies away without the sympathy of the community." Honkee and honker fly better together. Interdependently.

Today's ImproveMINT

Rely on each other on your team
to keep your leadership thinking in mint condition.

●

Filling In
Each Other's Gaps

Reading time: 3:24

Rocky Balboa, the struggling boxer in the movie *Rocky,* explains the apparent mismatch in the relationship he has with his girlfriend. Adrian is so very different from him — in personality, in behavior, and in habits. Yet together their synergy is exemplary. Rocky says: "I got gaps. She's got gaps. Together, we've got no gaps." Filling gaps and fulfilling expectations. That's what the most effective teams and team leaders do. They fill the gaps between individuals to create meaningful, interdependent, mutually-satisfying and productive relationships. They bring out the best in each other. They leverage each other. As Aristotle observed "the whole is greater than the sum of its parts." They strengthen each other with a synergy like the two horses that can pull 9,000 pounds MORE working together than they can working individually. They become more than a team. They become partners — inseparable and seemingly invincible — at least as long as they bond together with a synergy like this:

Meet Charlotte and Leonard. Theirs is a special relationship, one born out of mutual love that draws them from opposite ends of the county. Charlotte and Leonard, married but not to each other, meet nearly every day to make beautiful moves together. Their individual spouses don't mind that Charlotte and Leonard arouse and excite the other, often sweeping the other off his or her feet. Their rendezvous is a closer encounter of another kind where the only romance is their love for rhythm and grace, precision and poise. They are ice dancers— a dynamic duet, filling each other's gaps full. They complement each other's individual performance more than simply compliment on each other's individual performance. Their individual energy erupted into a synergy, the kind of synergy that spawned dynamic duets that dazzled and delighted movie audiences back in the day when Fred Astaire had his Ginger Rogers. And Ginger Rogers had her Fred Astaire. Spencer Tracy had his Katharine Hepburn. And Katharine Hepburn had her Spencer Tracy. Humphrey Bogart had his Lauren Bacall. And Lauren Bacall had her Humphrey Bogart.   And of course, Rocky had his Adrian and Adrian had her Rocky. Those dynamic duos filled the gaps full with, by and for each other. They balanced out each other in much the same way a pianist plays with both hands together in harmony. As famed composer Johanne Sebastian Bach observes: "It's not the autocracy of a single stubborn melody on the one hand and not the anarchy of unchecked noise on the other. No, it's a delicate balance between the two. That is an enlightened freedom."

That enlightened freedom —balanced and embolden—is the mark of every leader who brings together a synergy of talent, each reinforcing the other in a symphony of cooperation not a cacophony of competition. Together they lead each other toward higher horizons and toward a higher calling. Who could ever forget Rocky's mating call: AAADREEEANNNNN! And Adrian's response: ROCKEEE! They fulfilled each other's need to be loved and to be needed so they could LEAD their lives. Together. Each complementing the other. Each filling the other's gap.

Today's ImproveMINT

Seek complementary relationships
to keep your leadership thinking in mint condition.

●

Affirm Long Before You Inform

Reading time: 3:26

Bleeding and screaming, the 5-year-old girl tries in vain to fend off her growling attackers after she inadvertently wandered into a pit-bull dog pen. Her mother, panicking at the screams, flees into the pen like a hawk. She sweeps up her frightened and bitten daughter into the safety of her arms. "Ssh, Ssh, Ssh, it's okay now," her mom coos. She rushes her daughter to the security of a nearby bench, far away from the now locked dog pen. "You're okay. Momma's here for you. Ssh, Ssh, Ssh." But to no avail. Her little girl continues to cry. The louder her mom tries to comfort her daughter with an affectionate "Ssh, Ssh," the louder she cries. And the more she cries the faster she bleeds. The crying and bleeding seemed to get worse just when the ambulance arrived.

The trained medical first responder took the opposite tact. He confronted the situation first rather than comforted the victim. The emergency response leader first confirmed the reality of the situation as the frightened and injured little girl had just experienced it. "Wow, look at all that blood on your arm. I'll bet that really hurts, doesn't it?" Then the medical first responder knelt down and looked into the little girl's tearful eyes and gently asked: "Can you help me?" The little girl nodded. Her screaming diminished. "I think together we can stop that blood," he said while handing the girl a compress. "Just press this down on your arm while I bandage your other arm, okay?" The girl took the compress pad. She stopped screaming. He held the girl's arm and stated in a matter-of-fact tone: "Hey you are doing a great job for me. I knew you could stop that blood and you did!" Soon her bleeding stopped. So did her crying. The little girl was under the leadership (a.k.a. influence) of a trained first responder who knew that the way to initially treat a trauma victim is to first retreat into their world, to see the situation from their eyes, to feel their pain as they are feeling it. In initially confronting more than simply comforting her feelings , the first responder did much more than persuade the girl to stop crying. He influenced her to process her feelings, make sense of her feelings, and ultimately take control over her feelings.

The medical response leader unveiled a critical skill of all effective leaders —leveraging his emotional intelligence— to feel the pain the girl was feeling and to empathize with her situation. Expressing his emotional intelligence with more empathy than self-serving sympathy, he validated her feelings and in the process validated her. Then together they validated a process, working together—care giver and care recipient—to regain stability and create a new reality.

That's what leaders do. They help others cope and hope without discounting the reality of the situation or diminishing the impact of the circumstances—no matter how vicious the proverbial dogs or how painful their bites in whatever situation they are facing right now.

Leaders can focus on the moment to better define today confine yesterday and refine tomorrow. Real leaders in real time help others process their reality. Now. Leaders are always in the kNOW. Now! (See Afterward, page 260: *Savor your Leadership Mints NOW!)*

Today's ImproveMINT

Validate the situation others are facing
from their point of view
to keep your leadership thinking
in mint condition.

●

Mint 47

Parlaying Your Golden Eggs

Reading time: 3:12

A braham Lincoln, visiting wounded soldiers during the Civil War, leaned over the hospital bed of one injured soldier and asked: "Is there anything I can do for you? The soldier, not recognizing the president of the United States at his bedside, asked Lincoln to write a letter for him to his mother. The soldier began dictating. And the President began writing. "Mother...I am dying...." Abraham Lincoln knew his role as a Servant Leader: to foster a supportive environment for his troops. Effective leaders like Lincoln know the value in long-term productive relationships that aren't limited to job descriptions, reporting structures or organizational charts.

How can you apply that kind of Servant Leadership? Follow Larry, the Leader. Larry is more than a mid-level manager in a manufacturing plant. Larry is also a Servant Leader unencumbered by job descriptions or organizational charts. Larry still telephones Doug once a year to wish him well on his birthday even though it has been more than 10 years since Doug worked directly for Larry. "That phone call makes me feel really important," said Doug, who works in another part of the same company.

As a leader who cares about people, Larry's reputation precedes him wherever he goes. He knows that today, thanks in part to him, there are many geese throughout the company laying golden eggs of increased productivity and profitability in various departments. So how come there aren't more Larry-The-Leader types in the work-a-day world guarding the golden eggs and encouraging others to lay their own golden eggs? The short answer according to leadership development research: Too many would be leaders discount their feelings and end up undermining their leadership potential. Showing you care is the most important trait of any leader, notes British military historian John Keegan. Writing in his book *The Mask of Command.* Keegan says CARING is more significant than:

> (2) Knowing what to do
> (3) Rewarding behavior
> (4) Taking action or
> (5) Providing example.

And for those who would dismiss this caring aspect of leadership as too "touchy feely" consider that Keegan wrote more than 20 books on war, not exactly a "touchy feely" topic. Indeed caring for your people does impact the bottom-line as former Chrysler chairman Lee Iacocca asserts in his biography:

> *"In the end all business operations can be reduced to three words: people, products and profits. People come first. Unless you've got a good team, you can't do much with the other two."*

After all, the most effective leaders realize that gaining insight and understanding with others results from "the reciprocal action of men (and women) where feelings and ideas are renewed, the heart enlarged, and understanding developed," according to author Alexis de Tocqueville in his iconic book *Democracy in America.* President Abraham Lincoln practiced that kind of democracy, that kind of feeling, that kind of "reciprocal action" of, for and by the people. He cared. As a Servant Leader, he cared enough to preserve (read pre-serve) the golden eggs that enrich today and enlighten tomorrow. Just ask Doug.

Today's ImproveMINT

Care about your employees
to keep your leadership thinking in mint condition.

Mint 48

Collaborating
To Play The 19th Hole

Reading time: 3:15

E ye-catching and eye disturbing: The large photograph in the company president's office looked about as out of place as a pants presser in a nudist colony. The photograph, festooned among the president's framed diplomas and certificates, featured a turtle perched atop a fence post. Nothing more. The turtle was paralyzed in fear. Unable to move. Nowhere to go but down. And no one in sight to help the turtle get down. "We all need a helping hand every now and then," said the company president, explaining his turtle-on-the-fence-post photo. "That turtle needed some help getting up there and now that turtle is going to need plenty of help staying up there or getting down from there."

From Me to We

That's why hard charging leaders reach out and collaborate with others. The most effective leaders are like highly competitive golfers. They chase that elusive ball around the course with a personal passion that requires extensive individual concentration for 18 holes. But they play the proverbial 19th hole, differently. They collaborate with others on that 19th hole. They listen to others on that 19th hole. They learn from others on that 19th hole. And of course they socialize with others on that 19th hole, known more formally as the clubhouse bar or restaurant.   That transition from —ME to WE — is the key behavior in the evolution of a leader. That evolution —from ME, The Competitor—to WE, The Collaborators—requires more humility, more deference, more understanding, more listening, and more emotional intelligence. That evolution from ME to WE requires the leader in you to first harness your personal feelings while you become more aware of the feelings of others around you. That evolution from ME to WE underscores the rich body of leadership development research documenting the value of relationships in driving your career success and job performance including these dated studies still relevant today:

1. A Stanford Research Institute Study found that 89 percent of management is dealing effectively with people.
2. The Bureau of Vocational Guidance at Harvard University found that 80 percent of all job failures are due to poor relationships between employees and supervisors and not problems with job responsibilities.
3. And a Carnegie Institute of Technology study found that poor social skills contributed in 95 percent of those who were let go from their jobs after 10 years or more seniority.

No wonder effective relationships can determine the profitability of the stock market as management guru Peter Drucker observed. Or even help a turtle exercise its options high atop a pole—with something more promising than a shell game.

Today's ImproveMINT

Share experiences after a project
to keep your leadership thinking
in mint condition.

●

Partnering Power: How Sweet It Is!

Reading time: 7:07

Author's Note: *As a reporter with The Miami Herald in 1975, the author met Jackie Gleason in Fort Lauderdale, Florida and learned a lesson in leadership from the famed comedian that he never expected. Jackie Gleason was honing his golf swing to host President Gerald Ford in a celebrity round of golf with legendary entertainer Bob Hope and the greatest professional golfer at the time, Jack Nicklaus.*

G reat One. That's what the television entertainment world called Jackie Gleason. And no wonder. After all, he hosted popular television programs in the 1950s-1960s that dominated the airwaves from *The Honeymooners* to *The Jackie Gleason Show* on CBS. His loud-mouth character – Ralph Kramden – became the most famous bus driver in New York City on *The Honeymooners.* In fact, the first time I heard Jackie Gleason's voice —live and in person—he sounded more like the boisterous and cantankerous Ralph Kramden who would blare at his wife in the TV sitcom: "Straight to the Moon, Alice."

Jackie Gleason was mad as hell and he sure wasn't going to take it anymore.

He stood about 30 yards away from me on the driving range at the Inverrary Golf Resort in Florida, site of the Professional Golf Association's nationally televised tournament that week. Gleason yelled at my associate —a photographer for *The Miami Herald*— to stop taking photos ("Hey Pal, not now!"). *The Great One* demanded to be left alone to concentrate on his golf swing. By the time I could intervene and introduce myself as something more than a pesky fan, I figured Ralph Kramden would also kick me "straight to the moon" when I requested an on-the-record interview for my newspaper. Maybe I would have to settle for one of his patented threats: "One of these days... POW!!! Right in the kisser!" Or more to the point maybe the future police chief in Smokey of *Smokey and the Bandit* movie fame would pull me over and give me a go-to-jail card.

But I was wrong.

In fact, two years before Jackie Gleason would play Sheriff Justice chasing Burt Reynolds speeding down country roads in his Pontiac Trans Am in the movies, he arrested me. At least he arrested my attention in teaching me a lesson in leadership. He caught me off guard. Jackie Gleason's leadership lesson surprised me especially after I saw firsthand how self-absorbed and arrogant he appeared to be based on his personal behavior during a practice round of golf. Forget emotional intelligence. Mr. Gleason, the Great One became the Grate One. He seemed to flash more emotional arrogance than intelligence, a malady that seems to inflict plenty of celebrities. I asked permission to follow him around as he played a practice round alone. He ignored me. He focused only on washing his golf ball. Then he climbed into his super tricked-out Rolls Royce golf cart and started driving away. I couldn't believe how oblivious he was to the world around him. But then Jackie Gleason surprised me. Abruptly — almost as an afterthought- he waved for me to follow him in my own golf cart.

"How Sweet It Is!"

"How sweet it is!" I found myself saying in mimicking *The Great One's* famous line that he usually uttered after sipping something stronger than coffee from his ever-present coffee cup on stage. Then I found myself saying "And away we go!" —another classic Gleason line. It was quite a show that I got to see up close and personal: Jackie Gleason—The Golfer. And then Jackie Gleason—The Surprising Leader. On the golf course, *The Great One* seemed to take on the persona of the characters he made famous on his television programs. He smiled like *Joe the Bartender* after hitting a solid drive. He pouted like *The Poor Soul* when he missed a putt. He drove his limousine-looking golf cart with all the pomposity of the haughty *Reginald Van Gleason III*—much to the chagrin of other residents of the Inverrary Resort that morning also playing on the private golf course they shared with Mr. Gleason. A few of those residents even chided Mr. Gleason for repeatedly driving over and around the stakes and ropes guarding the greens. Three of his miffed Inverrary neighbors, playing in the adjacent fairway, shouted at The Great One to keep his cart out of the roped area. Mr. Gleason played deaf and played on. He was on a mission and nothing would defer him —not aggrieved neighbors or even a nosy reporter.

"And Away We Go!"

Jackie Gleason was lost in his own world, oblivious to everything around him except the golf club he held in his hand. He played quickly and deliberately. Alone. At times, he seemed to play as if he were running the table in a pool game with the same bravado and bravura he did playing Minnesota Fats in the movie *The Hustler* 14 years before. This was his 34th straight day playing or practicing his golf game to get ready for his match with Bob Hope, President Gerald Ford and Jack Nicklaus. After he finished his 11-over par round, I asked Jackie Gleason The Golfer about the first golf lesson he ever took. I told him how much I enjoyed watching him take his first golf lesson on his TV show with Art Carney in *The Honeymooners*.

In the comedy sketch, they were trying to learn to play golf from an instruction book. Gleason is standing in the kitchen with his driver while Art Carney reads from the how-to book. "It says here you have to address the ball," Carney reads. They both look perplexed. They are not sure how to address the ball. Then Carney takes the club away from Gleason and slowly bends over the ball and says: "Hello Ball." After I laughed at the memory of that skit, I complimented Mr. Gleason, but *The Great One* —the man who grew up poor and wound up rich and famous with an ego and bank account that seemed to get bigger every year—surprised me. He immediately deferred. "Well, that's all Carney, a genius." I was surprised at Gleason's acknowledgement of his partner's talent, especially given the arrogant behavior I just saw on the golf course and especially the way Jackie Gleason clearly exercised his creative license hogged the spotlight in front of the TV cameras and consistently marginalized Carney's character in their comedic skits. Check the TV situation comedy history books and you'll find Gleason's character never called Carney's character (Ed Norton) by his first name even though Carney's character always called Gleason's character (Kramden), by his first name — Ralph. As a viewer, I got the feeling that Ralph Kramden didn't want to let his guard down. I also got the feeling that Jackie Gleason's superiority as a self-defense mechanism was not too far from the way Jackie Gleason saw the world off stage in real life.

Yet from that complex bundle of emotions that I saw up close and personal — Jackie Gleason, The Surprising Leader — emerged. The *Great One* taught me a critical leadership lesson that resonates in particular with business partners and teammates in general — especially where one partner/teammate dominates: ***Value your partner or teammate especially when they work in your shadow. Remember they are holding the light that lets you shine.*** Without them, you are in the dark. With them, well... lights, camera, action. And Away We Go. How sweet it is!

Today's ImproveMINT

Credit the value of all partners
to keep your leadership thinking in mint condition.

●

Mint 50

Parlay Your Pygmalion Power

Reading time: 3:32

General Douglas MacArthur took off his own Distinguished Service Cross the day before a planned battle in World War II and pinned it on his battalion commander. "I'm confident you will earn that Distinguished Service Cross when you lead your men into battle tomorrow," MacArthur predicted. Not if. When. He did. And they were victorious.

Leaders "pre-ward" their followers What's a "pre-ward?" Same as a reward except a "pre-ward" is presented BEFORE an expected behavior or performance. A "pre-ward" ups the ante in personal expectation to an act of faith in others that can turn the ordinary into the extraordinary. A "pre-ward" can be something like the title or label you give to a group or an individual. A "pre-ward" could be the teacher who calls her students "scholars" or the football coach who calls his players "student athletes." A "pre-ward" can change the dynamics of a relationship.

Consider the patient who caught the hospital technician off guard with a "pre-ward" while he was routinely drawing a blood sample. The patient asked: "How long have you been a Care Giver?" The technician was surprised. No one had ever called him a Care Giver before. Nurses and doctors and social workers might use the term —Care Giver—to define themselves but not a medical technician, he thought. But then the technician began to come to life. He broke out of the cold stone of his job function. He breathed a new sense of purpose. And he smiled at his newly perceived value he was bringing to others beyond a simple diagnostic test. Do you have too many cold statues working for you? Then bring them back to life. With your own act of faith in them. With your own "pre-ward" to parlay your Pygmalion Power. You'll recall, Pygmalion was a king who longed for companionship and love, according to Greek mythology. (See page 208, Mint 80). He was also a sculptor who created a statue of a beautiful woman. He believed thoroughly in the statue. He loved that statue unconditionally. His conviction for the statue impressed Aphrodite so much that the Greek goddess of love brought the statue to life. Leaders in the real world can indeed invigorate their employees in a like — if not such a dramatic—manner. But first leaders have to realize their employees are not their employees. With apologies to Kahlil Gibran:

> *Your employees are not your employees. They come to work for you but they are not necessarily of you. And though they are with you, they belong not to you.*

Maybe that's why the most effective leaders develop compacts more than contracts with their employees:

- Compacts—mutual agreements—empowering more than employing.
- Compacts—mutual agreements—focusing on the possibilities not the impossibilities.
- Compacts—mutual agreements—sparking an unlimited performance mind-set.

And compacts sealed and delivered personally. With Pre-wards.

Today's ImproveMINT

Foster faith in others
to keep your leadership thinking in mint condition.

Mint 51

Valuing Your Vulnerability

Reading time: 3:53

You just got that big job, that promotion, that major account. And now you are feeling on top of the world. Invincible. You are the King or Queen of the corporate jungle. Hear ME roar! You feel like an elephant: the largest living land animal on earth with no natural predator. You sense the awesome power of an elephant as the 10 to 12-ton weapon packing 50,000 muscles used in war during the Roman Empire. So huge. So strong. So unconquerable. And yet so vulnerable. So vulnerable that the elephant's best friend in the jungle is the egret — a small bird that rides on the back of an elephant eating flies and other insects that "bug" the elephant's sensitive ears.

The elephant and an egret are reputed to be Mother Nature's Odd couple. They feed off each other's vulnerabilities and ironically they both become stronger. Think of that Odd Couple—the egret and the elephant—as a metaphor for the symbiotic relationship between the most effective leaders and their followers. After all, the most effective leaders do not mask their vulnerabilities no matter how strong or how influential or how mighty others think they are. In fact the most effective leaders readily acknowledge their own weakness. They selectively lower their guard to listen more carefully, to learn more comprehensively and ultimately to lead more productively. And in the process, they ironically get stronger. Leaders realize the more vulnerable they are the more real they can be. They know the more real they are, the more trust they can build. And they find the more trust they build, the better they can lead. (See page 138, Mint 52.) Being vulnerable can make a team more viable as one leader in a large company noted: "In meetings with staff, I try to be the first to say that I'm wrong about something. I have to be vulnerable first." The more vulnerable the leader the most engaged the staff. The most effective leaders understand the more they bare it—the better they can bear it—the better they can sense the working environment and perform accordingly. Even Charles Lindbergh embraced the value of vulnerability when he became the first to fly solo over the Atlantic Ocean and land on cover of TIME Magazine in 1927 as its first Person of the Year. And Lindbergh did it in part because of his vulnerability where he could more readily sense the elements during his 33 hour, 3,300 mile flight. He eschewed putting windows in his plane's cockpit even though windows would have made the plane more aerodynamically sound, more fuel efficient, longer ranged and safer (protecting his charts from literally flying away.) But Lindbergh did not want to be insulated— and isolated– from his surroundings. He wanted to be vulnerable and ultimately more viable.

With more vulnerability, he could feel what he could not see flying virtually blind into the oblivion of the night ahead and over the blackness of the Atlantic Ocean below. He thought the more he could feel the outside world the more he could think and the better he could fly into the history books. That's why the most effective leaders figuratively strip down to toughen up —much like the Sioux Indians would wear only a loincloth when they hunted Buffalo from their horses. With their bare legs they could grip the horse more securely and therefore shoot their arrows more accurately. Your sense of vulnerability can become an empowering capability that acknowledges among other things —the elephant in the room.

Today's ImproveMINT

Leverage your vulnerability
to keep your leadership thinking in mint condition.

Mint 52

Getting To Know You
Up Close & Personal

Reading time: 3:28

Anna's song in *The King and I* — *"Getting to Know You, Getting to Know All About You"* —could be the anthem of the most effective leaders. Those leaders don't have to study the research that says the MOST important leadership skill is taking a sincere personal interest in your employees. They already know it. They also know it is more productive for them to understand their followers than it is for their followers to understand them, as author Garry Wills notes in his book *Certain Trumpets*.

Forget the touchy/feeling stuff. There's a bottom-line, performance-driven significance to that Getting-to-Know-You, Seeking-to-Understand-You focus on followers. That bottom-line, stemming from an up close and personal team building initiative, virtually doubled the size of the United States, according to historian Stephen Ambrose. In his book *Undaunted Courage,* Ambrose notes that Captain Meriwether Lewis and Second Lieutenant William Clark of the U.S. Army developed and practiced a Getting-to-Know-You Seeking-to-Understand-You strategy with their staff of 35 volunteers. Ambrose cited that focus on the individual interests, talents and dispositions of their volunteers as "outstanding leadership" in driving the success of their 7,000 mile expedition in 1804. Lewis & Clark developed what Ambrose called an "intimate" insight into each staff person's skills and behavioral tendencies. And that insight evolved "into a tough, superbly disciplined family." If you look up the definition of —intimate— you'll find "a warm friendship developed through a long association." Of course, this is not the buddy-buddy, let's-have-a-beer together friendship. This is a workplace relationship that puts work in its place —in context. Leaders put work in its place —in context —in establishing a Getting-to-Know-You, Seeking-to-Understand-You   working   relationship. To get intimate, leaders have to figuratively bare themselves in front of their followers. They disrobe. They let go. They are open. They hide nothing. They are vulnerable. (See page 136, Mint 51). The more the leader reveals about herself or himself personally, the more their followers are likely to follow their lead. And then progressively, the more their followers will disclose meaningful tendencies in their own heart and soul that a leader can better leverage on the job for their mutual benefit. Then when the most effective leaders come to know their followers even more "intimately" they can better execute the fundamental act of a leader, according to historian James MacGregor Burns in his book *Leadership*:

> *"The leader's fundamental act is to induce*
> *people to be aware or conscious*
> *of what they feel,*
> *to feel their true needs so strongly,*
> *to define their values so meaningfully,*
> *that they can be moved*
> *to purposeful action."*

Moving people to purposeful action begins with the Getting-to- Know-You Seeking-to-Understand-You as author Dale Carnegie observed in his seminal book, *How to Win Friends and Influence People*. The more you are intimately interested in your staff — in their lives in and out of work— the more your staff will be interested in your mission the more engaged they will be in your vision and the more aligned they will be in your team's achievements.

Today's ImproveMINT

Get to know your staff personally
to keep your leadership thinking in mint condition.

●

Mint 53

Investing Together in a Mutual Trust Fund

Reading time: 3:23

Unexpectedly, the executive director showed up at the summer camp her organization sponsored. She made the rounds, inspected the facilities and noted the cracked window, the torn screen and the dirty walls. Then the executive confronted the camp director with the infractions. In a few hours the camp facilities were back in working order. Meanwhile on the other side of the lake, the executive director of another sponsoring organization showed up unexpectedly at their summer camp. She made no rounds. There was no inspection. She visited with the camp director and then together they walked randomly through the camp grounds and visited with other camp counselors without any predetermined itinerary or "rounds." The facilities were in good working order. No cracked windows. No torn screens. No dirty walls.

The evidence is clear: To get good performance, leaders don't have to inspect it. They have to EXPECT it. Of course that flies in the face of the well-worn adage that management gets what management inspects more often than what it expects. Yes, but that's all it gets. Compliance. No more. However, leaders with Great Expectations get even greater results--more than they expected and much more than they could ever inspect. With these Greater Expectations—with this focus on trusting another to perform well—come an even greater sense of personal responsibility, continuous improvement and a bond of trust. "Few things help an individual more than to place responsibility upon him and to let him know that you trust him," said noted author and educator Booker T. Washington. Grounded in that sense of responsibility, trust is the thrust of a quality-driven consistent performance. That kind of deep-seated mutual trust develops OVER TIME. It's a mutual trust that is sown more than sewn—grown day in and day out OVER TIME—not something stitched together IN TIME. It's a mutual trust sown with a variety of seeds including these nine leading behaviors from Stuart R. Levine and Michael A. Crom in their book *The Leader in You:*

1. *Recognize people.*
2. *Include them.*
3. *Encourage them.*
4. *Train them.*
5. *Ask their opinions.*
6. *Praise them.*
7. *Let them make decisions.*
8. *Give them the freedom to work as they see fit.*
9. *And convey your belief in their abilities by getting out of the way.*

The more leaders and followers trust in each other the more heightened and heartened they work together. They trust in living up to each other's expectations. They trust in fulfilling their responsibilities to each other. They trust in each other's individual expertise and tested capability to get the job done. Together they invest in a Mutual Trust Fund with each other FOR EACH OTHER. Together, their trust continually provides what leadership professor and author Warren Bennis calls a "lubricant that makes it possible for organizations to work." Without an inspection.

Today's ImproveMINT

Build trust to keep your
leadership thinking in mint condition.

●

Mint 54

DARE To Be Humble

Reading time: 3:54

General Colin Powell, then the nation's top military officer, kept a special phone line in his office that only he would personally answer. He gave the phone number to people he trusted would call him to keep his ego in check, to make sure he was staying connected to the real world, to make sure he knew when he was naked wearing the Emperor's Clothes. All leaders have their version of a Hotline to act quickly to divert a crisis, but how many leaders like General Powell have a PERSONAL Hotline — let's call it —a *SNOTLINE*—to help them avert a personal crisis? How many leaders would ask their friends to critique their behavior and alert them to what they can't see for themselves—like the proverbial snot hanging from their noses? Installing that *SNOTLINE* took humility, discipline and fortitude. With that deeply-developed sense of humility evolves a wisdom that helps a leader become even more real. Even more authentic. Even more humble and therefore even more engaging and even more potent as a leader.

Leaders dare to be humble.

As Norman Vincent Peale noted: "People with humility don't think less of themselves. They just think about themselves less." How can you become more humble with greater wisdom and character, in real-life situations? Let's scan the history books for real-world examples of leaders who dared to be humble:

- Booker T. Washington, the author and educator, was walking along 42nd Street in New York carrying a heavy suitcase. A stranger offered to help him carry the suitcase. They walked together and chatted. "And that was the first time I ever saw Theodore Roosevelt," Washington recalled years later. Leaders dare to be humble.

- He stood in the lobby as a capacity crowd streamed into the concert hall to hear the famous pianist. An attendant thought the man had not seen the "sold-out" sign and said: "I am sorry we have no available seats." The man nodded politely and said quietly: "May I be seated at the piano?" The man was famed pianist Arthur Rubenstein—the main attraction that evening. Leaders dare to be humble.

- The most effective leaders leverage their sense of humility as a teaching tool. An elderly lady came on board a train. She was carrying a large basket. There were no vacant seats. She finally reached the back of the train. The man in the last seat on the train rose promptly and gave the lady his seat. Immediately 20 men were on their feet offering the man his seat. "No gentlemen, if there was no seat for this old lady there is no seat for me." The man was General Robert E. Lee. Leaders dare to be humble.

- The man lit a cigar. The lady sitting behind him on the train chided the man: "You are probably a foreigner and do not know that there is a smoking-car attached to the train. Smoking is not permitted here." The man quietly threw away his cigar. Later the conductor told the woman that she had mistakenly entered the private car of General Ulysses S. Grant. Leaders dare to be humble.

Today's ImproveMINT

Hone your humility
to keep your leadership thinking in mint condition.

Mint 55

Get Off Your Buts

Reading time: 2:58

D r. McCoy and Mr. Spock are reunited on the starship for the first time in years in *Star Trek The Motion Picture*. McCoy—the affable people-oriented physician -- sniffs at Spock—the cold, aloof, analytical half human science officer: "You are as warm as ever and you haven't changed." And Spock, his voice dripping with equal sarcasm, retorts: "Nor have you changed, doctor, as your continued predilection for irrelevancy demonstrates."

Friction is the natural by-product when obstinate personalities clash. But without friction there would be no real power. Everything would quite literally slip away. So the most effective leaders do more than simply grease the points of friction in their organizations. They leverage it. They recognize feuding like that between McCoy and Spock —born in personality differences and bred in high-stress work environments—is bound to happen in any organization whenever and wherever highly intelligent, ambitious, opinionated people come together. And leaders know it is more productive to deal —more than duel —with people who brighten the room every time they leave it.

No wonder the most effective leaders embrace the notion of the wit who said: "It's not the ups and downs of life that bother me. It's the jerks." How do you deal with those jerks? It's too easy to find the negative in any situation, too easy to find a flaw, too easy to change the tone of discussion from upbeat to beat-up, and too easy to say, "Yes....but..." That's why the most effective leaders get off their "buts!!!" They conquer conflict with something more than the standard "Yes....but" mantra. They turn their 'buts" into 'ands." They weave together torn and tattered feelings into a quilt of understanding sewn with a degree of respect for each other's point of view and their right to their personal opinion.

- Instead of "BUT-ting" in and defending their point of view with a phrase that rolls off their tongue virtually at will— "Yes, but..."They respond: "Yes, **AND.**"

- Instead of "BUT-ting" in and challenging others directly with a "But, what it really means is," they say diplomatically: "**AND**, it could also mean."

- Instead of "BUT-ting" in and flatly rejecting another's opinion with a blunt outburst: "You're wrong," they say— "You're probably right, from your point of view. **AND** there might be another way to look at this that would also make sense to both of us."

- Instead of "BUT-ting" in-and defending yourself with a phrase like "You don't understand" the most effective leaders take the sting out of that charge by saying, "**AND** help me to better understand your concerns."

Leaders embrace conflict rather than merely brace for it. Conflict can sharpen your thinking knives. Welcome conflict, Abigale Adams — the wife of the President of the United States at the time— told her 10-year-old son who would become President of the United States. Mrs. Adams said: "The habits of a vigorous mind are formed in contending with difficulties." Conflict is the gadfly of thought," John Dewey, the education reformer, noted. "Conflict is a sine qua non of reflection and ingenuity. It stirs us to observation and memory. It instigates invention. It shocks us out of sheep-like passivity."

But in dealing with conflict—make no 'buts' —about it.

Today's ImproveMINT:

Keep an open mind. Say AND not BUT
to keep your leadership thinking in mint condition.

●

Balancing Act:
Preserving Relationships

Reading time: 2:56

Conflicting priorities. They go with the territory for all leaders. No wonder 64% of 1,800 executives in a Booz & Company survey cited "too many conflicting priorities" as their biggest frustration. What can you do when those conflicting priorities keep you up at night? Get away from it all. Go for a bike ride, at least in your mind. Pump some life back into your workday. And steer some balance back into your life. Think of your company or organization as if it were a wheel on a bicycle. And think of each of the 28 spokes (or 32 or 36) around the rim of your wheel as if they each represented a different constituent, a different stakeholder, a different public — each depending on the organization. Each makes demands on the organization and on you. If you tighten the spoke for investors and their demands for increased dividends, you might loosen the spoke for less costly health care. Then your rim—like any organization pulled and tugged in contradictory directions—surrenders its balance. And you are out of control.

That's why the most effective leaders are always seeking to balance their rims and regain or maintain that coveted control. Leaders seek to stabilize an organization's momentum and strengthen the integrity in its true course. To balance a rim, bicycle shops use a machine called a "TRUING" wheel. How appropriate! Leaders seek a true balance 24/7. That's why the most effective leaders always carry their own "spoke wrenches" of sorts in their pockets. They treat all spokes on their organization's wheel—all groups dependent on the organization—with a sense of fairness if not equanimity. They serve the needs of one group without compromising the needs of other groups. They use their "spoke wrenches" to maintain their ideal wheel balance with thoughtful, careful, even intimate care in serving all constituents fairly and equitably.

Yes, intimate care.

That sense of intimate care is clearly evident when you consider the name of the part of a bicycle spoke that is threaded into the rim. It's called a "nipple." How appropriate since it is through that nipple that the rim's strength and stability is nourished to cope with the bumpy roads of life and business. Nourishing all 28 nipples with proper balance requires considerable vigilance and discipline. If one is tightened then another reciprocating spoke is loosened and adjusted. Balance is in the balance. So the next time you are confronted with conflicting priorities, the next time you feel you are losing your balance, the next time you feel like your organization is wobbling out of your control, stop. Take a breath. Make the adjustment on your own "truing" wheel with a YQ, a Yield Question (See page 29, Mint 7) designed to maintain the equilibrium —the overall balance in your relationships with others especially in times of stress and confrontation. For example consider these Yield Questions that teachers might use in preserving a balanced relationship even while disciplining their students, as listed in *Teaching with Love & Logic* , a book by Jim Fay & David Funk :

- What would you like to happen?
- Would you like my thinking on that?
- Is it possible that?
- How do you suppose that might work out?
- What do you think I think?
- Would you like to hear what others have tried?

Today's ImproveMINT
Balance the needs of all groups
to keep your leadership thinking in mint condition.

●

Mint 57

Coloring Your World
From Bland to Grand

Reading time: 3:41

Angrily waving her hands, the vice president of human resources fumed during a talent review meeting. Her colleagues were complaining again that there were too many introverts under review as future leaders of the organization. "Why don't they get it?" she thought to herself. "Introverts are critical to our success." She felt like flinging a raw egg at someone. Instead she thought of something even more compelling, even more convincing: why not throw a dozen eggs at those executive whiners? And that's exactly what she did at their next meeting. She let her colleagues have it. And they ended up with the proverbial egg all over their collective faces.

The vice president made her point with what proved to be a meaningful demonstration: diversity is the key to talent development and the bland "eggs" are critical in developing a diverse, grand workforce. The vice president's persuasive demonstration began with a carton of a dozen eggs. Half of them colored like Easter eggs and the other half left shell white. "Of course we all want more of these kinds of leaders in our company." She pointed to the color-shelled eggs. They represented the super stars in a company, the best and the brightest. "So how do we get more of those vibrant, creative, colorful eggs in our corporate basket? With these," she said, pointing to the bland white shelled eggs. "Bland can be grand. In fact, we can't really optimize our colorful employees without hiring more of these so-called bland employees." Her colleagues winced in disbelief. Some figured this whole demo must be some kind of spoof. Maybe it was April Fool's day. Nope. She was earnest. And now some of her colleagues were wondering if all this focus on eggs had her brains scrambled somewhere. Or at least fried.

Undeterred, the vice president of human resources explained the critical leadership advantage of the neutral white shells in coloring Easter eggs: Opposites attract. The dye is mixed with vinegar. The dye is negatively charged. The vinegar is positively charged. So the neutral egg shell is the catalyst for the opposites to attract. Therefore, bland is grand. It is precisely BECAUSE the white-shelled egg is bland that it can lead the positively-charged vinegar to interact with the negatively-charged dye. That interaction gives birth to a plethora of spectacular colors -- GRAND colors that we celebrate at Easter. "Without these so called bland eggs we would not have so many grand eggs in our company," deadpanned the vice president of human resources. "We need the eggs. No matter what color they come in. Even no color." Besides Bill Gates, Mahatma Gandhi and Abraham Lincoln are among the many so-called bland eggs—introverts—who proved stellar leaders, she noted.

Then the vice president cited a scene from one of her favorite movies that reinforced her point on the power of eggs-elent relationships. In the final scene in *Annie Hall*, Woody Allen tells the story of a guy talking to a psychiatrist: "Doc, my brother's crazy. He thinks he's a chicken." Doctor replies: "Well, why don't you turn him in?" Guy says: "I would but I need the eggs." Then Woody Allen says in a voice over: "I guess that's pretty much how I feel about relationships. You know they are totally irrational and crazy and absurd. But I guess we keep going through it because most of us need the eggs." And so do leaders need the eggs. All the eggs. Even those with no color. Bland can be grand.

Today's ImproveMINT:

Value your introverted leaders
to keep your leadership thinking in mint condition.

●

Mint 58

Feeding the Birds
To Seed Your Message

Reading time: 5:22

Leadership is for the birds. At least that's how one company president observed as she scanned the executive suite. "There are 12 vice presidents in this company and no two of them are alike," she said to her visitor. "They're all birds of a different feather." Those birds, flying throughout your organization, are as different as Eagles, Peacocks, Doves and Owls. That's why the most effective leaders know they have to feed these birds differently in order for them to perch together on the same branch to achieve the intended goal:

- **EAGLES** celebrate proven results.
- **PEACOCKS** relish personal anecdotes.
- **DOVES** require congruence and conformity.
- **OWLS** seek documentation.

How do leaders discern the differences in their birds that comprise their staffs? They observe their different behaviors in routine matters.

- **EAGLES**, a.k.a. Cholerics, take charge.
- **PEACOCKS,** a.k.a. Sanguines, are the life of the party.
- **DOVES,** a.k.a. Phlegmatics, are calm and composed.
- **OWLS**, a.k.a. Melancholics, are methodical and gloomy.

Let's see if you can identify your dominant bird style as you read through the following scenarios. Then think how you would have to adapt your own behavior to coach or lead a bird of a different feather. Let's examine how differently each of these birds would react to these different situations—from recording a cell phone answering message to waiting for an elevator to waiting for a table in a restaurant to playing golf together.

Cell Phone Answering Message

Eagle: "I'm   not   available   right   now. Leave a message. I'll call you back."

Peacock: "Hey great to hear from you even though I am not here right now. I can't wait to get back to you. Hope you have a super day."

Dove: "Gee, I'm sorry I wasn't here to get your call. I will call you back just as soon as I can."

Owl: "Leave your number at the beep. You will have exactly 65 seconds from the sound of the beep."

Waiting for an Elevator

Eagle: "Let's go. C'mon. I haven't got all day. Step on it."

Peacock: "Hi, Bill. How about those (sports team)? They were something last night. Say why don't we have lunch later this week? Can't wait to tell you who I am bringing to the party this weekend."

Dove: "I could always take the stairs. It is only two flights up."

Owl: "The elevator is on the 16th floor. It will take 45 seconds to get down here. I can walk the two flights up in 30 seconds. It is smarter to walk."

Waiting for a Table in a Restaurant

Eagle: "A 40-minute wait! Are you kidding? Let's get out of here. I am not waiting 40 minutes for a table."

Peacock: "A 40-minute wait! Great! What a chance to check out the action in the bar. Hey, isn't that Judy over there?"

Dove: "A 40-minute wait? Well, it could be even longer at that other restaurant. Why don't we just make the best of it here?"

Owl: "A 40-minute wait. We are 9th on the reservation list. There are four tables right over there, working on their desserts. I calculate that we will be seated in 33 minutes."

Playing Golf in the Same Foursome

Eagle: "We're next on the tee. Let's go. I'll swing away first. You guys keep an eye on the ball."

Peacock: "Hey, look over there on the 9th green. That's Laura. Haven't seen her in a long time. She looks great. Remember the time Laura...."

Dove: "There's no one behind us. We can take our time. Maybe we can see Laura in the clubhouse later."

Owl: "Looks like we can finish 18 holes in less than 4 hours today. We should beat the rain by about 30 minutes at the rate we are playing."

The leadership lesson is clear: The most effective leaders adapt their coaching style, their speaking style, and their mannerisms to mirror the style of each individual on your staff.

- If you're an Eagle and you are always focusing on results, then stop. Take a breath. Share a story with your Peacock. Reassure your Dove. Credit the data your Owl presents to you.

- Likewise if you're an Owl and you are always seeking data, then stop. Consider the results with your Eagle. Relish a story with your Peacock about gathering that data. Compliment your Dove on his or her organizational and planning skills.

Each of the birds on your staff or in your audience may sing a different song but it is the effective leader who parlays their staff's individual strengths and complements their individual singing to align in harmony. In fact, it is the most effective leader and most persuasive public speaker who adapts, adjusts and develops "full-fledged" credentials to treat each bird differently based on their individual needs.

And so the leadership lesson is clear: Think of yourself as an adaptive bird feeder when you are coaching others or delivering a speech. Feed all four birds—the Eagles, Peacocks, Doves and Owls – the way they want to be fed (with results, anecdotes, comformity or documentation). Then you will have them eating right out of your hand with your leadership that is —for the birds.

Today's ImproveMINT

Adapt to other personality styles
to keep your leadership thinking in mint condition.

Mint 59

Staying in Touch
With Your Humanity

Reading time: 3:42

Baking bread from scratch is a therapy as much as a hobby to this corporate leader. It's Saturday morning. The pounding in the kitchen gets louder and louder and LOUDER! The vice president is home working in his kitchen—with a rolling-pin. He is pounding, pushing, pulling, pummeling the dough into delicious bread. Of course, it would be so much easier and more efficient to bake bread in a machine. Less mess and fuss yet not as much pure fun and joy. After all, making bread from scratch feels so much more satisfying, much more productive, and much more creative.

To this vice president, baking bread from scratch feels like being a sculptor, shaping the dough, filling in air holes and adding value overall to a lifeless wad of flour and water. Then suddenly it comes alive — seeming to rise from something more than just the yeast. Indeed the dough at his fingertips seems to rise as if he were performing CPR on the chest of the Pillsbury Doughboy, kneading him back to life and infusing him with a new found sense of personality if not humanity. A bit far-fetched? Not really. After all, the Making-Bread-From-Scratch model of leadership resonates in Cliff Stoll's book *Silicon Snake Oil*. He cites the perils of too much technology invading our personal lives. Predictable, you say, until you realize that Stoll is an astrophysicist. His viewpoint is counter-intuitive to our expectations of a Techy and therefore even more poignant and pregnant. When you surrender manual work to a machine, you lose what Stoll calls "the ritual, the sense of accomplishment, the feeling of being a part of the process." Stoll notes that the bread will taste just fine--if a bit too refined-baked in a machine. But you miss the best parts of baking bread: *"...the feeling of flour between your fingers, kneading the dough, punching the   air bubbles, finding a warm place for it to rise. Your friends' grins at the dinner table compliment you, not a machine."*

Of course technology is a keen resource but the most effective leaders periodically unplug from the grid. They realize what you lose in efficiency you can gain in effectiveness. They don't need to rely on WiFi. They sense they can connect more fully with a simple "hi" face to face that is more rewarding and personally satisfying. That's why leaders fight off the urge to surrender to technology, no matter how strong the pull of their Smart Phone that quite literally anchors their being. The most effective leaders still find value at times in noodling WITH others instead of Google-ing by themselves.

The most effective leaders affirm that at times the human touch can be more productive and powerful in the clutch than any machine. That 's the message in the story of chess playing robot that President Abraham Lincoln often told whenever someone questioned Ullysses S. Grant's ability to lead the army during the Civil War. The chess-playing robot beats a celebrated player twice. The celebrated chess expert cries foul at the machine. He wags his finger at the automaton. But then upon closer inspection of the robot he finds something even more disturbing. The losing chess player exclaims in a very derisive tone: "There's a man in it." Exactly. Technology works best when there is a human in it or behind it. So too in kneading bread or leading others.

Today's ImproveMINT

Express your need for human interaction
to keep your leadership thinking in mint condition.

●

Mint 60

Beware of Spraying Praise Like Perfume

Reading time: 3:28

Oh, Mrs. Cleaver you look so very nice today, gushed Eddie Haskell in the 1960s television program *Leave It To Beaver*. The teenager's sugar-coated voice oozed with a specious sap of insincerity. Eddie Haskell sprayed praise as if it were some kind of exploitive perfume that choked the air. He splashed his gratuitous smile and unctuous politeness on anyone and anything in killing his victims with faux kindness.

Do you know any Eddie Haskell's in your organization? Worse yet, are you falling into the Eddie Haskell trap of sugar-coating your relationship with your boss? After all gratuitous praise (a.k.a. brown-nosing) can become a weapon to stun and stunt others who hold a more powerful position over you. As Sigmund Freud noted "When someone abuses me I can defend myself. Against praise I am defenseless." How can you defend yourself against the Eddie Haskells of the world? Instead of praising, first consider appraising. When you appraise something —like a diamond— you evaluate its worth, significance and value based on specific criteria (cut, clarity, color). In appraising more than simply praising, effective leaders define, differentiate and distinguish others based on specifics, based on a sincere appreciation of the particular.

Leaders learn to be terrific they must be specific. "Good job" is too general a compliment. Add a specific trait or behavior that complements the compliment. "I really liked the way you organized the project and followed through. Good job." That compliment ON the job is a complement TO the job. It completes. It fulfills. It feeds a particular appetite not a general hunger. It smacks of sincere appreciation not flattery. As Dale Carnegie observed: "Flattery is from the teeth out. Sincere appreciation is from the heart out." Flattery is about as satisfying as fast food: filling but hardly fulfilling. No wonder nearly all employees suffer psychological malnutrition, according to Dr. David Schwartz, author of *Getting What You Want*. In a survey of 6,600 employees, 97 percent said they don't get as much appreciation on the job as they think they deserve. Indeed the ability to praise effectively is an under-utilized leadership skill that may be undermining the leader as much as the neglected employees. "The brilliant, efficient individuals who cannot warmly thank, compliment and commend their people will always fall short of their full potential as leaders," writes Perry Smith in his book *Taking Charge*.

How can you more accurately appraise others? How can you more specifically praise others? Begin by appreciating others.

- When you appreciate something you tend to nurture it, to grow it, to "make something more profitable," according to the dictionary.
- When you appreciate others, you add value to them.
- When you appreciate others, the leader-in-you takes stock of them individually. You invest in them personally.
- When you appreciate others, the leader in you appraises their work more fairly and frankly. Specifically. Specially. Sincerely.

And when you appreciate others you treat them with the dignity and respect that Eddie Haskell could never swallow.

Today's ImproveMINT

Be specific in appreciating others
to keep your leadership thinking in mint condition.

Mint 61

POWER LUNCH!
Beware of Feeding your Ego
Reading time: 2:42

Celebrating a successful product launch, the vice president hosted a lunch for 20 members of his team. Everyone munched on great-tasting sandwiches between celebratory cheers at their favorite deli. After a while, everyone was full of good food and good laughs. Then, the waiter arrives with a second round of sandwiches for all 21 people at the table. The staffers were astonished. "Who ordered all this," asked a couple of the team members in unison? "Well, I did," chimed the vice president. "You all deserve it. Job well done." It didn't matter to the vice president that no one at the table wanted another sandwich. Neither did the vice president as it turned out.

This afternoon's Power Lunch had little to do with feeding his staffers. It had more to do with the vice president feeding his own ego. So he ordered another round of sandwiches. Just because he could. The vice president seemed oblivious to the negative reaction from his staffers for the extra sandwich. So much for his sense of emotional intelligence. And so much for his power-packed inflated view of himself and his expense account that turned a celebration into a confrontation.

We all know managers who abuse power and seemingly aren't even aware of it. Their emotional intelligence is so low they see their world only through their narrow point of view and only in their terms. They don't know what they don't know. If they knew they might echo poet Robert Burns lament "Oh, what some power the Giftee gives us to see ourselves as others see us." But seeing ourselves as others see us is difficult, especially in wielding power in the workplace where sycophants too often find a welcome mat in the leader's office. As author Jeffrey Pfeffer notes in his book: *POWER, Why Some People Have It and Others Don't*:

"It's tough for those in power to see the world from others' perspectives, but if you are going to survive you need to get over yourself and your formal position and retain your sensitivity to the political dynamics around you."

Pfeffer, the professor of organizational behavior at Stanford University's Graduate School of Business, has studied leaders for 30 years. He writes that "it's hard work to keep your ego in check, to constantly be attentive to the actions of others." Especially when you're hungry for more than food.

The leadership lesson is clear: The next time you're hosting a celebratory luncheon consider also ordering a big slice of Humble Pie. And don't forget to check your ego at the door.

Today's ImproveMINT

Keep your ego in check
to keep your leadership thinking in mint condition.

●

Mint 62

PISSING People Off!

Reading time: 3:18

H ave you pissed off anyone today? You will —if you're a leader. Take it from General Colin Powell, former chairman of the Joint Chiefs of Staff and former Secretary of State:

"Being responsible sometimes means pissing people off."

After all a dog doesn't bark at a parked car. Leaders on the move will always summon critics like these:

In Politics

The Chicago Times called Abraham Lincoln's Gettysburg Address in November 1863 "silly, flat and dish-water utterances" that must "tingle the cheek of every American with shame." The London Times said the speech was "ludicrous, dull and commonplace."

In Music

Beethoven, the great pianist of his time was criticized for playing "noisy, unnatural, over-pedaled and confused." Beethoven even criticized fellow pianist Mozart: "Mozart's touch was neat and clean but rather empty, flat and antiquated."

In Science

Rocket inventor Bob Goddard was personally attacked in the New York Times for seeming to "lack the knowledge ladled out daily in high schools." In 1926, six years after the New York Times editorialized that rockets could not operate in space, Goddard blasted himself into the history books—and the Times critics into pundit oblivion—with the successful launch of the first rocket.

In Journalism

Al Neuharth, the founder of USA Today, parlayed criticism into giving life to the nation's first newspaper with flashy graphics and short snappy stories. He said that without the steady barrage of criticism from other media "we (the newspaper, USA Today) probably would have been stillborn. Instead people wanted to see this newborn kid (especially since it was) being denounced as a demon."

The most effective leaders see criticism as a catalyst for continued action and reaction that stirs their creative juices. Hell hath no fury as an artist scorned. Consider Michelangelo. He painted 20 nudes in the *Last Judgment* for the Sistine Chapel. A Church official criticized its "indecency." Michelangelo retaliated by painting the Church official in Hell, his face flanked with donkey ears. The Church official pleaded with the Pope to erase his face in Hell. The Pope wittingly responded that he could intercede only for those in Purgatory. But the Pope had no power over those in Hell.

So be glad when you hear someone calling you a #%&#&!!!! After all, as Edmund Burke, the British statesman noted "he who opposes me and does not destroy me strengthens me." That criticism that initially stings your ears and pierces your heart may spark you into a new creative arena at best or confirm your leadership position at the very least. So go ahead. Get ahead. Be a leader. Piss someone off today!

Today's ImproveMINT

Embrace criticism as a catalyst for personal growth to keep your leadership thinking in mint condition.

●

Mint 63

Self-Control:
The Ultimate Power

Reading time: 3:21

S torming into his boss's office, the vice president fired away in a staccato of criticisms that verbally shredded the company president's heritage and history. Unperturbed, the president calmly waited for him to catch his breath and said quietly yet firmly: "Let's talk." And then in a softer consoling whisper, he said: "I'm listening." Finally the onslaught of criticisms abated while the president stayed calm and in self-control. The vice president continued to vent albeit more professionally. Finally the irritated vice president began adopting the president's demeanor, calm and in self-control.

Most of us would have lashed out in self-defense at anyone making accusations and deriding our judgment. But the president—with his emotional intelligence sharpened— leveraged his sense of poise under pressure to diffuse the situation and ultimately take control. No wonder that the most effective leaders consistently demonstrate that self-control is the ultimate power. In fact, the most effective leaders embrace the notion of poet Alfred Tennyson that: "Self reverence, self-knowledge and self-control—these three alone lead a life to sovereign power." That why leaders are more effective exercising their self-control than their position power.

With self-control leaders engender a more comprehensive, more meaningful, more productive relationship with others that spawns more discretionary behavior, energy, creativity and productivity. With self-control leaders can more fully influence others without having to command them or worse yet control them. With self-control, a leader is more apt to yield power to others, develop more teamwork, and in the process ironically gain even more personal power. Power stems from within — in the heart not in the hand. And when a leader exhibits more self-control, he or she is also more fully conquering his or her own fears. Effective leaders know that British historian Lord Acton didn't get it quite right in 1907 when he said power tends to corrupt and absolute power corrupts absolutely. But power is not the culprit. Fear is. Fear tends to corrupt and absolute fear corrupts absolutely.

Fear Corrupts

Consider author John Steinbeck's portrayal of the king in *Short Reign of Pippin IV.* The king says: "Power does not corrupt. Fear corrupts. Perhaps the fear of lost power." Indeed, fear is the culprit in the quest for power as author Jack Gibb observes in his book *Trust*: "People who want power, control, influence, and status usually want these states as a defense against fears of being impotent, insignificant, and inferior or under arbitrary control of others." Maybe that's why President Abraham Lincoln said:

"Nearly all men can stand adversity
but if you want to test a man's character,
give him power."

Yet with self-control, power emerges from calming down not blowing up, from seeking within not searching out. After all, power grabbing executives ironically weaken their leadership muscle, as philosopher Lao-tse noted: "Force is followed by a lack of strength." Don't force your power. Enforce it —with your self-control.

Today's ImproveMINT

Leverage your self-control
to keep your leadership thinking in mint condition.

●

Mint 64

SCORE
Don't Get Sore
Reading time: 6:24

Bill is late again for your staff meeting and you're ready to explode. Somehow you bite your tongue. You maintain your composure. But then after the meeting, after everyone else leaves the meeting room, you confront the tardy employee—your best sales producer. Your frustration gets the better of you. You explode with a flurry of accusations:

> "Bill, the next time you're late for a staff meeting, we are going to have a serious talk about you finding another position," the boss barked. "I just can't have that kind of cavalier behavior around here. I don't care how many sales records you break."

The boss stormed out of the meeting room. Bill was stunned. But the boss's outrage backfired. Bill's sales performance got worse after their confrontation even though Bill did report to the next staff meeting on time. The boss had won the battle but seemed to have lost the war.

What happened?

The boss let his temper undermine his leadership capability and his team's production dropped. He got sore. But in reprimanding employees, the most effective leaders don't get sore. They SCORE. They SCORE with a five part process that states the *Situation,* cites the *Consequences*, poses the *Options*, sparks a *Response,* and then assesses the effectiveness of the intervention with an *Evaluation*. SCORE is an acrostic that helps you exercise your emotional intelligence and take charge over your emotions in tense situations that challenge your leadership.

Situation

(Be specific about this particular behavior in this particular situation. State the facts and focus on your feelings.)

"Bill, I'd like to talk to you about being late for this morning's staff meeting. I know that things come up and we all have to juggle a lot of balls, but it concerns me when I notice that you have been consistently late for our last four staff meetings."

Consequence

(Describe the specific impact of the behavior.)

"Bill, when you are not here on time for our staff meetings, we all lose. The rest of the staff loses out on learning by example from the top performer you are. Keeping commitments is a critical behavior in our success and when you're late for a scheduled staff meeting you and I miss an opportunity to teach that critical skill of keeping your commitments to our entire staff. And of course when you're not on time, you may miss valuable information that could help you sell even more aggressively and more profitably."

Options

(Ask for the employee's help in creating alternative behaviors for a successful result).

"I wonder what suggestions you have that would help you to get to the staff meetings on time in the future?"

Response

*(Collaborate on above options,
and then collectively agree
on a clear response that will result
in the expected new behavior.)*

"Okay, then you are going to make sure your sales reports are in the day before the meeting so that you don't have to spend so much time that morning getting ready for the meeting. Is that right? And I will be sure to get you the key agenda items at least three days ahead of the meeting."

Evaluation

*(Assess and acknowledge
the specific newly exhibited behavior.)*

"Bill, I really liked the way you got that sales report into me the day before our meeting and I know we all benefited from your being on time the following day for our staff meeting."

Use that five-step SCORE process and engage your emotional intelligence to play a key role in any conflict management situation. When you're facing a conflict like this, take a deep breath. Slow down. Take off the gloves. Invite collaboration. In developing your own SCORE-ing techniques—your own reprimand regimen—you'll leverage your emotional intelligence. You'll exercise greater self-control. You'll guard against your self-defense mechanisms to attack, to blame, to accuse, to judge and to impose. You'll harness your raw feelings so that you don't unleash your Pigeon Prowess—the downfall of many promising leaders—where you fly in, crap on your people, and then fly off in a flurry of My Way or the Highway dogmas. And you'll guard against breathing your own self-aggrandizing exhaust when bombast and bravura seemingly explode whenever the best and the brightest convene. John Adams virtually choked on the exhausting hot-air exhaust of his colleagues during the First Continental Congress in Philadelphia in 1774. Adams felt a lot of hot air blowing particularly INSIDE the building when he first took his seat with the same leaders who two years later would draft the Declaration of Independence. It seemed to Adams that the 53 other delegates each thought they were the sharpest saw in the shed. Just ask 'em. Each would whip his own hot air into every speech with heightened sense of bluster and braggadocio even on the most mundane of issues. That grandstanding made Adams very uncomfortable, according to historian David McCullough. In a letter to his wife Abigale, Adams noted that every man in the Continental Congress was a "great man—an orator, a critic, a statesman, and therefore every man upon every question must show his oratory, his criticism, and his political abilities." Adams thought all that verbal hot air marginalized the important work of the Congress, according to McCullough, and forced them to spend a lot of time spinning their wheels, exaggerating the trivial and delaying the real business. So many egos, so little time.   Adams was clearly frustrated when he sighed:

"I believe if it was moved and seconded that we should come to a resolution that three and two make five, we should be entertained with logic and rhetoric, law, history, politics and mathematics concerning the subject for two whole days and then we should pass the resolution unanimously in the affirmative."

Beware of breathing your own hot air and in the process burning out the spirit and initiative in others. Your people have sparkling ideas that need to be fanned. Not blown away. The most effective leaders fan the flames of extraordinary performance to help others SCORE.

Today's ImproveMINT

*Reprimand with emotional intelligence
to keep your leadership thinking in mint condition.*

Mint 65

Throw 'em a LIFE Line

Reading time: 3:34

After reviewing a proposed policy from one of his vice presidents, the company president groused: "I don't like it one bit." The vice president did more than defend his position. He got defensive. No one listened to the other. Finally, exasperated, the vice president stormed out of president's office, depressed and dejected. Meanwhile the president felt misunderstood and abandoned. Nerves fried. Egos frayed.

Just another day in the corporate boxing ring where punches are thrown sometimes below the belt. Or sometimes just because you have the upper hand. Whatever. After all, it's your budget. It's your company. It's your decision.

Yet those not in power are still determined to speak truth to power. No matter how bloody and battered we get, we still jab and jaw to get our ideas heard, understood and acted upon. Yet too often your ideas are dead on arrival unless you can pump LIFE into those proposals. LIFE is an acrostic for: Listen, Investigate, Feel, and Explore.

Listen

Resist your urge to be defensive or worse — argumentative—in the wake of initial criticism to your proposal. Be pensive not defensive. Listen with your eyes. Your eyes have 22 times the nerve endings your ears have. Be present in the moment. Don't let your thoughts wander off into planning your response. And keep your mouth shut. After all, saying nothing is the ultimate COMMAND of the language. As leaders we know that we are supposed to first seek to understand then to be understood as Stephen

Covey conveys so well in his *7 Habits of Highly Effective People.*

Investigate

   Probe with empathy. Stay calm. Seek to understand the specific criticism with a clarifying phrase like: "Can you tell me what specific areas you don't like about this new proposal? Practice what Socrates called *Koinonia.* In Greek, *Koinonia* means "the spirit of fellowship." In practicing *Koinonia* you dialogue without arguing and without interrupting and you celebrate the sense of community and the spirit of sharing.

Feel

   Confirm the critic's feelings. Acknowledge their point of view. Affirm the validity of their perspective—from their point of view. Then confirm that you really do feel what they feel. Rephrase their point of view until they acknowledge that they have been heard — until what they said and what you heard is virtually a "copy and paste" function, according to author Chip Bell. In his book *Managers as Mentors,* Bell notes "the mission of listening is to be so tuned into the other person's message that understanding becomes a copy and paste function from one mind to another."

Explore

   Explore the possibilities together. Stay open to continuous improvement. Reach out and throw your two life preservers —your ears—toward the other person. Then they may be more open to pumping more LIFE into your new ideas.

Today's ImproveMINT:

Pump LIFE into your proposals
to keep your leadership thinking in mint condition.

Mint 66

Climbing Down From Your Ivory Tower

Reading time: 6:14

Executives can easily be insulated and maybe even isolated from the average employee's world. High-powered executives daily are ensconced in chauffeured limousines, protected from the real world traffic and congestion. They live in spectacular homes in gated communities protected from the real world of crime. These high-powered executives work in palatial offices with breath-taking views, protected from the real world of life in a cubicle. There are no house keepers, nannies, chefs, or gardeners in the average employee's world. That's why a supervisor in a manufacturing plant was pleasantly surprised when he learned the president of their billion-dollar global company lived in a middle class neighborhood not far from the corporate headquarters. The company president had no chauffeur. And on any given Saturday afternoon the company president could be found at home mowing his own lawn. Why did this millionaire choose to live more like one of his average employees than like most other company presidents?

Access. "All employees need to know they can talk to THEIR company president any time they need to," the company president explained. The president taught a valuable lesson to all leaders: climb down from your ivory tower and get as close as possible to your front-line employees. Then you will learn what is really going on in your company with greater detail and documentation than a status report written days or weeks later. Of course the company the president led had a well utilized Open Door Policy. But this president opened his door even wider. And in the process, the president leveraged his understanding and appreciation for what average employee lives were like —on and off—the job. His sense of personal humility and vulnerability—no gated community and no chauffer— engendered a working environment of mutual trust. That trust between employees and management has been instrumental in the company operating for more than 100 years without a union and without any employee strikes. "Without employees who feel valued, you don't have a company, you have an organization," the president said. A company is more focused around people while an organization is anchored around processes and systems. It's instructive that we focus on people when we say that we are having <u>company</u> over for dinner.

The word <u>company</u> stems from the Latin word for bread (panis) and so the most enlightened leaders break bread with their employees. Together they build a mutually beneficial relationship that nets a productive and profitable company. That's why the most enlightened leaders know how, when and where—and by whom—their bread is baked, buttered and served. Of course there are all kinds of security issues today that would undermine this wide of a wide open Open Door Policy. But the concept of climbing down out of your Ivory Tower to get a real feel for the real world is still viable.   What can you do as a leader to become even more accessible and approachable to your employees? Consider these six ideas to get you even closer to your company, to your people:

1. HOBBY SHOWCASE: Invite all employees to showcase their hobbies in the cafeteria. Have a day dedicated to Pottery or Model Airplane hobbyists etc. Stage an all-afternoon barbeque. Invite C-Suite leaders to take a shift barbequing and grilling for their employees. Invite leaders of the company to visit the exhibits and talk to employees during their lunch hours or before or after shifts so that production will not be affected.

2. COFFEE WAGON: Tour the manufacturing plants in a golf cart toting hot coffee and donuts. Serve the coffee and donuts at key stops just before the work day begins. You might have to get up at 4 am just like some of your employees.

3. RANDOM LUNCHES: Invite 6-8 employees at random for lunch with the president of the company. (Perhaps those who share the same birthdate or birth month).

4. RELOCATE THE WATER COOLER: Consider converting your main reception desk into a free snack bar for customers, employees, and management to interact.

5. CREATE A CORPORATE CAMPFIRE. Place a coffee urn in the middle of your most populated work area (attracting workers from next floor up or down) for a specific period each day and the coffee won't be the only thing brewing. Workers in sight often give leaders an insight.

6. FORM A CREATIVITY EXPLORERS GROUP: Invite all employees to informal brown bag lunches to discuss ideas on creativity.

Together these different employees from different departments become much like the different grapes from different vineyards in a Dom Perignon bottle of champagne. They interact together in a second fermenting process. They catalyze each other with an enriching sense of synergy. They bring out the best in each other. They break down the insulation—and often the isolation—of the C-Suite. And they drive each other. Chauffeurs need not apply.

Today's ImproveMINT

Stay in touch with the rank and file
to keep your leadership thinking in mint condition.

●

COLLABORATING

Leadership Mints
Extra Bonus

Following on pages 173-177
is a look behind the scenes
at the collaborative spirit
and emotional intelligence
of golf legend Jack Nicklaus
off the course.

Jack Nicklaus
On Fatherhood

Reading time: 11:17

You may know Jack Nicklaus – the famed Golden Bear– as the greatest professional golfer of all time. But I once got to know a very personal side of Jack Nicklaus light years away from the golf course. And in the process he taught me a lesson in personal leadership and in emotional intelligence that I never forgot: Get in Touch with your Feelings—especially off the job—so that you can better focus your performance on the job. It was 1973 and at 33 Jack Nicklaus was at the top of his game. The Golden Bear so dominated the professional golf world that three weeks later he would set the record for winning the most major golf championships-- a record that Bobby Jones held for 43 years, a record that Nicklaus is likely to still hold 43 years later in 2016, a record that includes an incredible 18 victories and an unprecedented 19 second-place finishes in major golf tournaments.

As a newspaper reporter for *The Miami Herald* in Florida. I worked out of the newspaper's West Palm Beach office just 9 miles from Jack Nicklaus' home in North Palm Beach. On Tuesday afternoon, July 24, 1973 The Miami Herald got a news tip from Good Samaritan Medical Center in West Palm Beach that Jack Nicklaus would be visiting the nursery ward to see his fifth born child (Michael) for the first time. My editor assigned me to interview the winner of both the Masters and the US Open just a year before and now the highest paid and most famous golfer in the world. I balked. I told my boss that this was a very personal moment for a dad and his newborn son and that a pesky reporter had no right butting in. Reluctantly, I entered the nursery ward with my photographer. And sure enough there is the Golden Bear —all alone—in front of a glass wall overlooking the newborns. There were no security guards

around him. No cameras. No entourage. No hangers on.
Jack Nicklaus stood all alone with his thoughts—and
feelings—for his newborn son. I stood about 20 feet away
hating what I was about to do: invade his
privacy. (I needed this job, my first out of college.) Finally, I
get enough courage to interrupt Jack's virtual mind meld
with his son through the glass wall into the nursery. I
introduce myself as a reporter and tell him that I'd like to
talk to him about being a dad, about seeing his newborn
son for the first time.

Nicklaus' famous blue eyes glazed over me. I could tell
he didn't hear a word I said. I backed off. He went back to
gaga-gooing at the window. Then I approached him
again. Once again, I told him who I was and what I was
doing there. I was hoping he'd throw me out. (At least then
I would have an excuse for my editors.) But Jack surprised
me. This time he looked directly into my eyes and
said: "Well, what do you want to know?" Then in the
corner of the room, I see a nurse standing with a wheelchair
ready to go. "I have the smelling salts if you need it, Jack,"
the nurse bellows. I am thinking this smelling salts
comment must be some code for alerting security. But that
didn't happen. Nothing I expected happened on this July
afternoon in South Florida. I expected Nicklaus to give me a
quasi-pep talk that his newborn son would grow up
disciplined, responsible and competitive etc. After
all, Nicklaus earned his Golden Bear moniker for his
ferocious style of play more than his blond hair—a ferocious
style of play that helped him already bag 11 of his 18 major
golf tournaments. He had already won four of his 6 masters,
three of his 4 US Opens, two of his 5 PGA Championships
and two of his 3 (British) Opens. That's why I was surprised
to hear Jack Nicklaus—the man with steel nerves who
consistently sank 12-foot putts for thousands of dollars—
saying that he felt "queasy in my stomach" when he saw his
newborn son for the first time. I was even more surprised to
learn that he fainted each time he saw his first four children
as newborns. He joked that he spent more time in the
recovery room than his wife, Barbara did after delivering

their third child, Nancy. At first, I thought Nicklaus was putting me on with all this talk of fainting. I thought he might be having a little fun with a rookie reporter. I made sure he knew I was quoting him. He clearly saw my notebook. Then I asked him why he would want his fans to know that he got sick to his stomach seeing his newborns for the first time. Nicklaus said: "It's a good human reaction to have." Jack Nicklaus clearly saw a teaching opportunity to help other dads get closer to their children, to help other busy executives make more time for their kids. The headline in the Miami Herald the next day said: *"Nicklaus Always a Jittery Dad."*

But 20 days later Jack Nicklaus had no jitters on the golf course. He won the PGA Championship and earned THE CREDENTIAL to become professional golf's greatest player. He surpassed Bobby Jones' record for most major championships. Yet, in another salute to his emotional intelligence as a leader in the world of fathers, Nicklaus recalls that same tournament generated his favorite golf photo of all time—ironically without a golf club in his hands. Jack is photographed carrying his then four-year-old son Gary on his shoulder. Gary came running out onto the 18th green after Jack had just finished the third round. Nicklaus embraced his feelings as a dad even while the nation had a spotlight on him as a sports hero. Nicklaus stayed true to his character, true to himself. His family is his priority even when everyone else is focusing on Jack. Likewise in deciding to grant an interview during such a private moment, Jack Nicklaus focused on inspiring other dads. He could have brushed off the reporter with a vexing "call my PR people for an interview." He didn't. He could have surrounded himself with an entourage of staff people. He didn't. Instead, Jack Nicklaus showed up wearing none of the trappings of his celebrity. Instead, the celebrity-golfer-turned-celebrated dad taught all busy dads a significant personal leadership lesson: *be true to yourself.* Be real. Thirteen years later, Nicklaus was still being true to himself, still unleashing his sharpened emotional intelligence, still focusing on the important not the urgent. Then on Sunday

April 13, 1986 when his fans were losing their minds in delirious joy of the improbable, 46-year-old Jack Nicklaus was methodically marching down the back nine recording a six-under par 30 to vault over eight other contenders and become the oldest ever to win the game's most prestigious championship, the Masters. When Nicklaus eagled 15 and came within 36 inches of a hole-in-one on 16 and then sank an 18-footer for a birdie on 17, *Sports Illustrated* magazine described the ensuing pandemonium: "Grown men climbed trees, children rode on shoulders, concession-stand operators abandoned their posts, all just to tear off a swatch of history." The crowd reacted with such a roar Nicklaus called it "deafening."

Yet he stayed focused and performed magnificently even though he was facing even more personal pressure off the golf course than most of the millions watching on television could fathom. Nicklaus also had to deal with a financial sword hanging precariously over his head as he played. His over-extended company was flirting with bankruptcy. But Nicklaus, exercising his emotional intelligence of a leader in knowing clearly what he valued, faced his financial woes head on. He was still putting a financial compress on his bleeding company when he struggled to an opening two over par 74 at the Masters. Just seven months before mastering the Masters in 1986, Nicklaus took over the reins of his troubled company from the professional business manager he hired to handle day-to-day operations. The professional business manager did a good job over the previous 10 years, Nicklaus insisted. But now they just had a difference in business philosophy. He wanted "to build an empire," Nicklaus told *Sports Illustrated*. "But I don't want an empire." Jack Nicklaus, like the most effective leaders, knew exactly who he was and what he valued. "What am I going to do with an empire? I've got five kids, a beautiful wife and I'm hoping on some grandkids. That's what I care about." Today Jack and his wife have 21 grandchildren and his company is on firmer financial footing. When you are comfortable in your own skin, you can adapt more readily to pressure situations and stay focused amid distractions. That's the leadership lesson that Jack Nicklaus taught us all. Likewise on the golf course he adapted against the odds. After all, he hadn't won a major tournament in six years or a Masters in 11. And when he came to the 1986 Masters Championship, Nicklaus was already saddled with a plenty of playing baggage: he missed the cut in three of the last seven tournaments. Yet Nicklaus —The Collaborative Leader—soldiered on, grounded in his strong sense of family and fortified in his own refined sense of emotional intelligence. Jack's mother was among the cheering crowd at the Masters for the first time since her son first played the Masters in 1959. Jack's sister was there for the first time ever to see her brother play the Masters. Jack's eldest son, Jackie, had a ringside seat to history-in-the-making as his dad's official caddy at the Masters. And that Sunday, Nicklaus had another family figure cheering him on—the memory of a 13-year-old boy who Nicklaus championed and celebrated throughout his bout with bone cancer until he died 15 years before.

To cheer up Craig Smith, the son of the minister who married Jack and Barbara, Nicklaus told the boy he would wear the teen's favorite colored shirt on Sundays on national television while playing in the final round of a golf tournament. Each Sunday Craig and Jack donned their matching yellow shirts as a tribute to each other. Their matching shirts created a bond that seemingly knitted their relationship even closer. Ten weeks after Nicklaus wore the yellow shirt and won the 1971 PGA Championship, Craig died. And so did the significance of wearing the yellow shirt until THAT Sunday 15 years later when Nicklaus rekindled those feelings of hope at the Masters in 1986. That Sunday he wore his emotions on his yellow sleeve again. That Sunday Barbara suggested —and selected—the yellow shirt for Jack who happens to be color blind. His wife always knew that he never needed to personally see colors. After all, Jack Nicklaus was always coloring the world a bit brighter for others to see and experience. Collaboratively. Like a leader. Even in a hospital nursery ward—to the surprise and delight of a nosy reporter.

●

COMMUNICATING
Part III

"If all my possessions

were taken from me,

with but one exception,

I would choose to keep

the power of communication,

for by it, I would soon

regain all the rest."

Daniel Webster,
Famed Orator,
Former United States Secretary of State

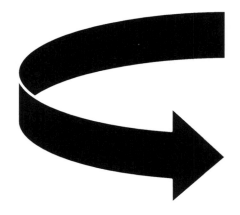

Mint 67

Confessions of a Listener: Father, I Have Sinned

Reading time: 3:01

Panicking beneath the weight of his own guilt, the eight-year-old boy crashed to his knees in the dimly lit phone-booth-like structure and whispered nervously: "Bless me, Father, for I have sinned. This is my first confession." The boy's voice cracked with embarrassment before he blurted through the darkened window of the confessional: "Oh Father, I have sinned. I played with... (gulp)(gulp). Nuts ...in my pants."

The priest raised his eyebrows —and then his voice— before growling at the boy: "Son, you did what?

The boy stammered: "Well, there was this pretty girl in my second grade class that I really liked," his voice trailing off in embarrassment. "Yes, yes go on," encouraged the priest. The boy fidgeted back and forth on his knees, swallowed, took a deep breath and finally explained: "Well I wanted to make her a necklace. Out of chestnuts. You know. You drill a hole in the chestnut and then string them together to make a necklace."

"Oh, Oh," acknowledged the priest in a comforting tone. But the boy heard the priest say "Uh-Oh," in a more scolding tone. The youngster finally summoned his courage and blurted out his sin: "I was walking to church one morning when I stopped to fill my pants pockets with chestnuts that I found lying all over the ground. I still made it to church on time. But when I knelt down in the pew, my bulging pants pockets exploded with chestnuts all over the wooden bench. It sounded like Fourth-of-July firecrackers were exploding all over the church! Oh, Father I sinned." Yes the youngster did sin. He committed the sin of not really listening. The boy heard the scolding "uh-oh, uh-oh" instead of a knowing "oh-oh." And the priest sinned too. He committed the sin of jumping to a false assumption that he was hearing another X-rated confession. At times, I've been just as guilty of sinning at listening. Maybe you have too.

- As a listening sinner, I have traded points of view rather than listening to the other's viewpoint.
- As a listening sinner, I have settled for a "duel-ogue" rather than a dialogue.
- As a listening sinner, I have concentrated too much on what I already knew to learn anything new.

But now, I have an even deeper understanding of poet Robert Frost's notion that the power of education is the ability to listen to almost anything without losing your temper or your self-confidence. I've learned the hard way: It takes courage and discipline to listen well. That's why the most effective leaders work every day at learning to be an attentive listener, a more active listener. These listening leaders focus first on restating the other person's point of view before adding their own point of view. They pray for the strength to become a more empathic listener, a confessor who can help others cope with hope. They learn to hate the sin but still love the sinner. No matter how loud the fireworks in a church.

Today's ImproveMINT

***Guard against jumping to conclusions
to keep your leadership thinking in mint condition.***

Mint 68

Listen: Do You
Want to Know a Secret?

Reading time: 3:36

SShhhh "Listen: do you want to know a secret?" Chances are you're humming that Beatles' song right now. But with all due respect to George Harrison's clandestine offer, the answer today for too many is: No. No. No. No! Too many people do not want to know a secret. That would mean they would have to LISTEN! And too many people say they are too busy to really stop and listen. Even if it kills them. Really? People would rather die than listen? No way you say. Consider the night the Martians invaded New York City and terrorized the nation. That night too many people heard that the Martians had landed in Central Park and yet too few really listened to the truth. They were too busy screaming in fear, no matter that the "Martians-Are-Coming" mantra was fiction, fable and/or make-believe. Yet millions of hysterical Americans believed this Halloween evening radio broadcast in 1938 was real.

Panic broke out across America! In Pittsburgh, a man returned home during the broadcast and found his wife with a bottle of poison in her hand crying, "I'd rather die this way than like that." No. No. No. They weren't really listening to the radio announcer's disclaimer three different times during the broadcast: **"You are listening to a dramatization of Mercury Theater's War of the Worlds with Orson Welles."** Too many tuned into their radios without really tuning it to what they were hearing. No wonder they seemed more deaf than deft in showcasing their listening skills. They were too quick to speak and too slow to listen. They were too quick to sing the *Sounds of Silence* as Simon & Garfunkel intoned: "*People talking without speaking. People hearing without listening. People* *writing songs that voices never share."* Too many struggle like the Midnight Cowboy in Harry Nilsson's song *Everybody's Talkin' at Me:*

"Can't hear a word they're sayin'.
Only the echoes of my mind."

The most effective leaders keep their ears wide open and their mouths relatively shut. Leaders embrace the notion of author Perry Smith, writing in his book *Rules & Tools For Leaders,* that listening is the most important skill of a leader. Listening is so important to our well-being as humans that hearing is the first of our senses to fully function—at just 23 weeks after conception when the human fetus is just 5.5 inches long and weighs 7 ounces! And listening is so important to the viability of our lives that our sense of hearing is the last of our five senses to die.

That's why Hospice advises family members never to assume that the dying person cannot hear. In fact Hospice says family members should direct their conversation to their dying family member even though he or she might not be able to verbally respond. They still hear you. It's instructive that your ears get larger as you age. It's as if Mother Nature is telling us to keep broadening your listening skills no matter how old you get with or without a hearing aid. In fact, listening is so critical that Helen Keller who was deaf and blind insisted that a sense of hearing was more important to keeping her in the "intellectual company of man." On Earth. Not Mars —if you are willing to listen critically; if you are willing to know a secret and if you are willing to lead, to act on something not merely react to anything.

Today's ImproveMINT

Sharpen your listening skills
to keep your leadership thinking in mint condition.

Mint 69

Becoming an "Eye-deal" Leader

Reading time: 3:43

Your eyes speak long before you do. That's why judges in ancient China believed so thoroughly in the eye as the portal to the soul. They donned dark glasses so that people in the court could not see what the judges were thinking. The judges knew their eyes spoke more loudly than their words.   That's why the most effective leaders make every effort to do more than simply make eye contact when speaking to others. They also make a visual handshake—personally and poignantly—with a specific person in the audience. Their eyes lock on to each other as intently if not as passionately as Tony eyes Maria across the dance floor in *West Side Story*. No matter what obstacles are in the way. In fact, author Bob Woodward was surprised to see how intently President Bill Clinton maintained eye contact while drinking a can of soda during an interview. At any rate, eye contact can be a trust builder that infuses others with strong bonds of loyalty and confidence.

General Robert E. Lee leveraged the insight of his eyesight during the Civil War and his weary soldiers could feel the warmth of his personality even in stark silence. One morning Lee mounted his horse and reviewed the troops in silence. No words. No applause. No cheers. The enemy troops were too close. Lee and his troops were forced to maintain silence. Yet they still communicated meaningfully and memorably with their eyes. Lee knew more than half of the soldiers he rode by would give their lives in battle later that day.   He stopped. Took off his hat and gazed silently at his soldiers in a personal tribute to their courage. Tears began welling in his eyes as he rode slowly past the troops. He then put his hat back on his head and rode away. Then a young soldier ran forward and said: "Any man who won't fight after what the General just SAID is a damn coward."

Leaders lead with their eyes. Your eyes are so integral to your ability to sincerely connect with others that even the statues of famous leaders reflect a special tribute to the eyes. Take for example the 11-foot wide eyes on each of the four Presidents of the United States carved into Mount Rushmore. Sculptor Gutzon Borglum chiseled large rectangular blocks of slightly raised marble into the white part of the eye, adding a life-like sparkle and an animated gleam to the 60-foot-tall faces of Presidents George Washington, Abraham Lincoln, Thomas Jefferson, and Theodore Roosevelt. French sculptor Jean Antoine Houston used the same technique to add life to his portrait statues. To enhance the white part of the eye, he left some of the marble slightly raised to better capture the light.

So too your eyes should sparkle and gleam as you capture the audience's eye as a leader in general and a public speaker in particular. Your eyes should sparkle like windows—windows into the soul as the proverb says. Classic movie buffs know that actor Gary Cooper's eyes sparkled on the silver screen. His eyes spoke more clearly, more cogently, more convincingly than his words. At least that's how fellow actor Lloyd Nolan evaluated Cooper's success after watching him film a scene in which Nolan felt that Cooper didn't do anything extraordinary. In fact, Nolan wondered what Cooper was being paid for. "But when you saw the rushes (the film shot that day), you knew," said Nolan. "Picture acting is all in the eyes." And so is communicating effectively and leading purposefully. It's all in the eyes. Just ask any "eye-deal" leader.

Today's ImproveMINT

Speak with your eyes
to keep your leadership thinking in mint condition.

Mint 70

Making LOVE To Your Audience

Reading time: 3:17

Making LOVE—Looking On Vitally Engaged—is a keen leadership listening skill that very few have mastered as well as Art Linkletter —an "eye-deal" leader extraordinaire. For 17 years on network television, Linkletter listened with his eyes and his entire face as much as with his ears and earned his friendly and funny reputation for conversing with people known more for their lack of attentiveness, their inclination to fidget and even cry. Yet Linkletter routinely calmed those 5 or 6-year-old youngsters and retained their attention. With his eyes.

Linkletter would kneel down directly in front of the child sitting in a row of chairs with three or four other youngsters. Then he would position his face up close—IN THE FACE— of the youngster during a popular segment of his *House Party* program called: *Kids Say The Darndest Things.* Imagine trying to quell the nerves of adults sitting on a panel for an interview segment under hot television lights before a national audience. Now think of a 5 or 6-year-old wiggling and twitching. But then a squirming and worming youngster would catch a glimpse of Linkletter's face making a visual handshake with him or her. Then the youngster would see those big friendly eyes homing in closer and closer and getting bigger and bigger until they loomed like huge lollipops. Those lollipop eyes seemed to get brighter and brighter as Linkletter bathed his face in a smile that seemed to get wider and wider until his smile felt like a warm blanket on a cool night. The combination of caring eyes and a warm smile helped the youngsters feel more valued, more protected, more safe. Now those hot lights weren't so hot any more. And those fancy cameras and the television audience were blocked from their view by this smiling face up close and personal. Now they felt they could even sit still long enough for this warm, friendly face to keep smiling at them and asking questions, much to the delight of the adults watching what was then the nation's longest-running day time television program.

Linkletter's lollipop-like wide eyes illustrates how the pupils of your eyes can expand 100-fold when you get engaged in something that interests you. That's why the most effective leaders use their eyes to increase their face value in their leading conversations in general and their public speaking in particular.

" Listening
is the first duty
of love."

The most effective leaders know their eyes and ears communicate more than their words or actions. That's why philosopher Paul Tillich said listening is the first duty of love and leadership legendary author Tom Peters says listening is the highest form of courtesy. When you listen with your eyes, you make others feel important. You add value to them. You bring out the best in them. That's what eye-deal leaders do: they bring out the best in others. With LOVE!

Today's ImproveMINT

Make LOVE (Look on Vitally Engaged)
to keep your leadership thinking in mint condition.

●

Mint 71

FLIRTing
With Your Audience

Reading time: 5:46

How do the most effective leaders leverage their public speaking skills to more fully engage an audience? They FLIRT!

- No, you don't have to share a furtive glance with someone sitting close to the lectern.
- No, you don't have to soften your voice in a sexy whisper.
- No, you don't have to bite your own lip in a moment of passion or run your tongue along your teeth at a delectable thought.
- No, you don't have to kneel down on one knee and plead ever so fervently with a member of the audience.
- No, you don't have to walk into the audience and softly waltz a finger across someone's cheek or touch someone so gingerly on the shoulder.

All you have to do is FLIRT.   FLIRT is an acrostic for five ways you can use your body language to get the audience to figuratively dance with you, to follow you—and your message—step by step: Feeling, Looking, Invoking, Roaming and Tasking.

Feeling

To feel your audience, reach out and HUG them. With Feeling. HUG stands for *Handily Use Gestures.* Let your fingers figuratively run through the hair of your audience. Let your audience feel what you are feeling through your fingers, hands and arms—through your gestures. Forget about yourself. Think only of your audience. Success comes when you focus on others, in speaking with them or in leading them. That's the experience of August Turk, the former CEO and founder of two highly successful businesses and the author of *Business Secrets of the Trappist Monks*. Turk says: "Every great leader knows or should know that the more they focus on making OTHER people successful rather than worry about their own success, the faster their own promotions will come."

Looking

Do more than look at your audience. LOVE 'em. LOVE stands for *Look On Vitally Engaged.* In flirting with your audience, the eyes say it all. (See page 185, Mint 70.) Maybe that's why Arturo Toscanini, the famed Italian orchestra conductor, would memorize long symphonies so that he could maintain eye contact with his musicians and infuse them with an energy and passion that enhanced their performance. Consider how masterfully Toscanini listened with his eyes, according to Dorothy Sarnoff, writing in her book *Speech Can Change Your Life*. "When Toscanini conducted for singers, the expression on his face was one of rapture. He listened with such ecstasy that they could not help out-singing themselves."

Invoking

Ask your audience for their help. Mohandas Gandhi could hardly walk to the podium. In fact he had to sit down as soon as he reached the podium. Seated, he spoke for only one minute on April 14, 1919. But his message was felt as much as heard. He touched their hearts and souls and invoked their allegiance to his cause with his personal appeal to : *"Take thought before you sign the Pledge (against unjust laws). But if you sign it, see to it that you never violate the Pledge you have signed. May God help you and me in carrying out the Pledge."* No doubt many in the audience saw and felt the commitment that an ailing Gandhi had for his message of freedom over tyranny and that his body language alone set the tone for the way the audience heard the text of the speech read to them.

Roaming

Think of the stage as a canvas and you are the artist. Dab a color here and move over a few feet and dip your brush with still another color. Don't settle for the single color you can paint while anchored to a lectern or podium. Pull your anchor. Push out from behind the lectern. Do what Elizabeth Dole did at the 1996 Republican convention. Speaking on behalf of her husband—Bob Dole for president of the United States— Mrs. Dole roamed. She left the podium, walked down a flight of stairs in front of the stage and roamed into the audience. Her body language spoke of confidence and conviction as she roamed toward specific individuals in the audience who played a role in her message. She literally walked the talk.

Tasking

Give your audience an assignment to more fully engage them. Be like the chief executive officer of a large industrial firm at the conclusion of a company-wide meeting on quality. He grabbed a chair and climbed on it and appealed to his vice presidents: "Repeat after me. I will listen. I will not shoot the messenger. I recognize that management is the problem." To better focus your intended message to task your audience consider using the Five Fingers Story Telling research technique developed by Karuna Ramanathan, a Lieutenant Colonel in the Singapore military. Your fingers can figuratively point you toward the most appropriate emotional hook for your story. Your pinky finger is the most vulnerable and therefore the source of stories battling back from a challenging experience. Your ring finger is symbolic of stories of relationships, love and integrity. Your middle finger is symbolic of situations spawning aggravation, frustration and despair. Your pointer finger helps you focus on a specific direction, destination or key point. And your thumb fosters positive "Thumbs Up" stories filled with exhilaration and achievement.

INTRO Your Audience

So in summary to win over your audience at your next speech, FLIRT with them. Or at least give them a meaningful INTRO— an acrostic that stands for Interest, Needs, Timing, Range and Objective. Use this INTRO process to engage an audience in a meaningful learning opportunity. INTRO is a process developed for the American Hotel & Lodging Association for its Certified Hospitality Educator program. The INTRO helped subject matter experts focus their teaching on the way adult learners learn. In this INTRO model, you construct an opening designed to capture the:

- **Interest** (appeal to the widest segment)
- **Needs** (targeted benefit of this information)
- **Timing** (how long do I have to pay attention)
- **Range** (of what will be covered) and the
- **Objective** (the goal and why is it is necessary to the audience success on the job and growth of the company.

With practice, the INTRO can be delivered in approximately 5-6 minutes. Think of your INTRO as a mouth-watering appetizer designed to whet your appetite of what to expect and why so that you can more fully digest the meal to come. To prepare your INTRO, start with your research. Then find a reference from the Internet or tell a story that introduces the topic to your audience in a meaningful and memorable way.   And FLIRT with a dash of your personality.

Today's ImproveMINT

FLIRT with your audience
to keep your leadership thinking in mint condition.

Mint 72

Smiling to Leverage Your Face Value

Reading time: 3:19

Passionately Jimmy Stewart kisses Donna Reed in the movie *"It's a Wonderful Life."* The producer and the camera crew were thrilled with the scene. But the scriptwriter complained the actors left out a whole page of dialogue. Frank Capra, the director, responded: "With technique like that who needs dialogue? Print it!" Their ensuing smiles beamed a palpable sense of exhilaration and energy. No wonder actors on and off stage, including the most effective leaders, know how powerful their smiles can be in leveraging their face value. They know a smile — the only thing you can't break by cracking—can soothe. At least many injured soldiers thought so. Imagine a hospital scene with 1800 injured soldiers. Florence Nightingale and her staff of 43 nurses administered smiles along the four miles of beds as if it those smiles were like so many vials of medicine. One soldier expressed the palliative sensations of her smile like this: *"She would speak to one and nod and smile to many more. We lay there by the hundreds. But we could kiss her shadow as it fell and lay our heads as the pillow against it, content."*

Florence Nightingale leveraged her face value—her smile—to affect even more people than she could personally attend. You don't have to be a Florence Nightingale to leverage your face value in the workplace. But you do have to be aware of the tool all leaders wield—their body language — to affect the behavior of others, to affect the well-being of others, to affect the productivity of others and maybe even to change history. At least Abraham Lincoln thought so. He was especially concerned about one aspect of his body language — his handwriting — when he was about to sign the Emancipation Proclamation. The President said his right arm felt almost paralyzed from shaking so many hands earlier that day. "If my hand trembles when I sign the Proclamation, all who examine the document hereafter will say: 'He hesitated,'" Lincoln told the Secretary of State who had brought the document to the White House for his signature. Lincoln forced himself to fight off the pain and signed the document with a personal strength in his hand and conviction in his heart that reinforced his freeing the slaves.

Beware and aware of how much your body language speaks for you and against you even before you speak. Yogi Berra, the baseball Hall of Famer, earned his nickname from the way he sat on the ground as a teen-age ballplayer with his arms and legs folded "like a yogi" between innings when there was no dugout or bench for the players. And now the world knows Lawrence Peter Berra famously as Yogi. His body language even spawned a cartoon namesake—Yogi Bear—in 1958 at Hanna Barbera Productions. Indeed, your body language speaks louder than you do. Consider the way Sir Walter Scott leveraged the body language of his opponent to win a debate. As a schoolboy, Sir Walter Scott regularly lost debates to a particular student. One day he noticed that his rival routinely fumbled with a particular button on his vest as he spoke. The next time the two debated, Scott found a way to remove the button from his competitor's vest before he spoke. Then during the debate, the more his rival fumbled for the missing button, the more he fumbled for words. And the more he fumbled for words, the more he fumbled away a new opportunity to leverage his face value. Actions always speak louder than words. Button down your performance to lead. With a smile.

Today's ImproveMINT

Increase your face value with a smile
to keep your leadership thinking in mint condition.

●

Mint 73

Arming Yourself With Body Language

Reading time: 3:09

S tanding on one leg like a sleek flamingo in front of more than 200 people, the vice president shared his vision for a reorganized department. He noted that managers in the department had been forced to stand on one leg because of recent budget cutbacks. No more. "Today I am announcing a reorganization of our department that will give more people two legs to stand on," he said, firmly planting his other leg on the stage with a loud bang. The flamingo disappeared. So did the doubt. And his audience applauded the news.

Days later managers greeted each other in the halls with The Stomp, reliving the experience of getting back on their proverbial feet. That stomping vice president had leveraged a key tenet of leadership: the power of your body language to clarify and amplify your words so that they are more fully heard, understood and acted upon. The Stomp —or some version of it—is a potent leadership tool that George Washington and Thomas Jefferson among other historical figures utilized in leveraging their body language. Washington relied on his body language when his troops were too exhausted, too frustrated, and too angry to listen to his words. His troops wanted to revolt over not being paid their back salary. Imagine telling your staff that you could not afford to pay them this week! The General knew it was futile to try to reason with his battle-worn and weary troops. Words weren't enough. He reached into his pocket and put on his glasses. Washington never wore glasses in public before. Historians tell us he was too proud to admit that his eyes were failing him. His troops were surprised to see their leader allowing himself to be less than perfect in public. Washington collapsed into a chair and said wearily: "Gentlemen I have grown old in your services and now I am growing blind." The guilt trip worked. The men chose not to revolt.

Thomas Jefferson also let his body language do most of the talking when he got up to make a speech at the University of Virginia.   Jefferson, who founded the University of Virginia after serving as President of the United States, was frustrated and angry. A gang of maverick students had taken over the dorms of the University and turned them into gambling rooms. Jefferson was so overcome with emotion, he couldn't speak. He simply sat back down in exasperation. The students-turned-gamblers heard his body language so loudly they restored the dorms.

Like Washington and Jefferson, the most effective leaders showcase their body language. They recognize what the deaf already know: that body language is even more telling, more compelling and more significant than sign language to people who are deaf.   As Lottie Riekehof, author of the *Joy of Signing*, observes:

> *"Deaf persons do not focus so much on reading each other's hands as they do on reading the face and the overall body language."*

And so the leadership lesson is clear: Let the flamingo in you STOMP on your stump. Memorably. And give your speech legs!

Today's ImproveMINT

Remember that your body speaks
louder than you do
to keep your leadership thinking in mint condition.

●

Mint 74

Stewing Ideas in Your Personal Crock Pot

Reading time: 3:24

When Dorothy in the *Wizard of Oz* first meets the scarecrow, she is mystified. Scanning the straw that passes for the scarecrow's brain, a confused Dorothy erupts: "But if you haven't got a brain, how can you talk? The scarecrow responds matter-of-factly: "I don't know but I've seen a lot of people without brains do a lot of talking."

Talking yes. Speaking no.

That's why the most effective speaker/leaders recognize the power in speaking more and talking less. After all, The Speaker (of the House) not The Talker is the third person in line to the presidency. Anyone can 'give a talk." No listeners required. But only an effective speaker/leader can speak —can deliver a speech—when listeners are not only required but engaged. Talkers simply sound off. Talkers like to hear themselves more than listen to others. Talkers like to run their mouths so quickly they often say something they haven't thought of yet. No wonder the discerning leader says talking and speaking are about as different to the spoken word as the microwave oven and the crock pot are to cooking. Talking, like fast food in a microwave oven, is ready for consumption in a few seconds. At the push of a button. Anytime. Anyhow. Anywhere.

Meanwhile speaking is like a gourmet stew, simmering in a crock pot of thoughts and ideas for hours and then stirred with years of experience and spiced with keen insight and expertise before serving. It's ready only at a specific time. And it is viable only until a certain expiration date. That's why many speaker/leaders prefer the slow and deliberate over the quick and quixotic. Emotionally intelligent leaders prefer the crock pot over the microwave. Thoughtful leaders need to stew their ideas and let them simmer IN rather than heat them up and let them sizzle OUT. After all, those thoughtful leaders literally have a speaking part to play with their audience:

They speak WITH
more than talk TO their audience.

The most influential speakers seem to feel what the audience is thinking and feeling. Leaders seem to be conversing with their audience on a two-way road of understanding where the most thoughtful and effective leaders regularly climb down from their Ivory Towers to breathe the people's air close to the ground. (See Mint 66, page 169). Leaders come to speak with—more than talk down to—their people. And they think like Sitting Bull.

Historians tell us that Sitting Bull earned his name for his deliberative thinking style. But once the Sioux Indian Chief made up his mind, once he completed his "sitting," he would 'bull" ahead unwaveringly. Sitting quietly —slowing down—enhances the precision of command in the most effective leaders who regularly throw their WAIT around, who regularly pack a dose of patience into their performance. You lose your sense of savoring the finer things in life when you eat quickly instead of dine leisurely. Slow Down. Think. Stew your ideas in your personal crock pot. Then have your say. With a lot more than straw for brains.

Today's ImproveMINT
Use a crock pot not a microwave oven
to keep your leadership thinking in mint condition.

●

Mint 75

Breaking Through
The Dam of Indifference

Reading time: 3:36

You are the subject-matter expert in your company, the sharpest saw in the shed. Yet every time you try to saw through a concept with a customer, those BLOCKHEADS as you call them, seem to get thicker and thicker the way they block you out of getting your message through. What can you do to cut through the indifference of those blocking out your message? And what can you do to help your audience more fully soak up your highly-researched, well-documented message? Stop sawing. Start watering. Slowly.

Forget trying to saw your way through a presentation very deliberately, rhythmically, factually, point by point, and case study after case study. Instead, turn your faucet of information on slowly and water only when the customer says they want to be cooled off with a fine spray of insight that refreshes. Yet too many over-zealous experts, filled to the brim with facts and figures, are too quick to flood their audiences with information that says more about the presenter's ego than about the audience's need to know. No wonder barrier-prone audiences will be just as quick to build a personal dam—a BLOCKHEAD—to protect them from your flood waters.

But there is hope. Your audience will open its dam if it believes the speaker's water (i.e. message) will easily flow into its own stream of personal interests, concerns and desires and will fill — and more significantly FULFILL—their own personal pipelines without polluting their values and beliefs. But how do you get into the flow of an audience's personal stream of consciousness? Seek to lead a discussion not manage a presentation. Focus on influencing not persuading. The word "influence" stems from the Latin word to "flow into." When you influence others, you flow into their feelings so fully that "they can be moved to purposeful action," as James MacGregor Burns notes in his seminal book *Leadership*.

When you influence others, when you flow into your audience's thinking, they sense your thinking as an extension of their own. They come to see your water as feeding and freshening their own quality of life. Then your audience comes to regard you more personally as a resource for their affirmation than just professionally as a source for your information. As a resource, you become a fountain of knowledge available to your customer when they are thirsty—on their terms. As a resource, you become contagious to others in a most favorable way. As author Mike Hyatt points out, "It's no coincidence that influence and influenza (the flu) come from the same root word. Real leaders are contagious. People catch what they have."

The leadership lesson is clear: To break through the dam of indifference, your role as subject-matter expert is to "infect" your audience and to help your audience realize just how thirsty they are. Then help them intelliGENTLY savor—not swallow—your SOLUTION, one sip at a time. Your audience will then sense the value in your solution and begin to turn on YOUR faucet wider and wider into the pool of your ideas. Then you will connect with your audience as if both you and your audience were swimming together in the flow of your mutual thoughts and streaming past those blockheads.

Today's ImproveMINT

Flow into the ideas of others
to keep your leadership thinking in mint condition.

●

Mint 76

Tuning In To WII-FM
Reading time: 2:36

Make a "you-turn" the next time you find yourself standing on a podium or next to a lectern. The most effective leaders realize they have to deliver the audience to the speech long before they deliver the speech to the audience. They tune in to what the audience is already attuned to—the most listened to personal radio station of sorts in the world, a personal radio station you're listening to right now: WII-FM *(What's In It For Me)*. Unless a leader answers that question —*What's in it for me?* —in specific detail, the audience will drift into la-la land and throw you out on your ear for not finding and tuning in to their ears. Consider this three-step approach to better deliver the audience to your speech:

1. Tune in to the same WII-FM station that the audience is listening to so that you can personally feel what the audience feels.

2. Weave those feelings – those threads of hope and despair—into a net of mutual understanding that surrounds the speaker/leader and the audience.

3. Tug ever so gently on that net of mutual understanding to pull the audience toward the speaker/leader –and into—the message.

Tugging on the feelings of others, the most effective public speaking leaders heed the advice of Benjamin Disraeli, the former British Prime Minister, "Talk to a man about himself and he will listen for hours." They transform the audience's feelings into poignant words — words that prick the heart and soul of each person in the audience, words that prick each of them so personally, so passionately and so powerfully. And in that Pricking Process, the audience and the speaker/leader become one. They are woven together into the same net of pain and pleasure, frustration and fortune. One becoming the other. In the Pricking Process:

1. The speaker/leader becomes the spindle from which the audience's feelings unravel.

2. The speaker/leader becomes the conduit from which the audience's energy flows.

3. The speaker/leader becomes a human transfer station that keeps the audience awash in its own value system.

The speaker/leader "perceives a vapor arising from the people condenses it and then passes it back to the audience in a flood," as former British Prime Minister William Gladstone once observed.

Use that three-step Pricking Process to become an even more effective leader and an even more engaging "CommUnicator." With the accent clearly on the "You" 24/7.

Today's ImproveMINT

Tune in to the specific interests and concerns
of your audience
to keep your leadership thinking in mint condition.

●

Speak Loudly &
Carry a Big Sledgehammer

Reading time: 3:11

Mad. Angry. Infuriated. The founder of the McDonald's hamburger empire was fuming. Ray Kroc was so hot that you could have grilled a Big Mac on his forehand. Well, sort of. The Golden Arch patriarch wanted his store managers to spend more time with customers in the front of the store and less time on bookwork sitting on the wooden chair in the office in back of the store. He sent each store manager a hand saw and a message: Saw off the back of your chair. Apocryphal or not, the story illustrates Kroc's persistence to continuously improve performance, a persistence that is the crux of leadership, a persistence that emboldens, a persistence that embodies, embraces and espouses a can-do, will-do, spirit, energy and drive. Sometimes the most persistent and effective leaders speak loudly and carry a big sledgehammer of sorts to make their points visually, memorably and of course most persistently:

- Consider the persistence of the newly named chief executive officer at a glass manufacturer. He used a sledgehammer to literally obliterate the past in order to create a new corporate direction. In front of a hundreds of sales staffers, he pulverized more than $1 million of decorative glass that had made the company successful. But the market was changing and the company had to head into a new direction.

- Consider the persistence of the chief executive officer of a leading technology company who spent his first day on the job — in the parking lot. Painting. He took off his coat and tie, dipped a paint brush into a gallon of black paint and painted over the well-marked executive parking spaces, beginning with his name. The leadership lesson is clear: Sometimes leaders have to speak loudly and carry a saw, a sledgehammer or a paint brush to wake up an audience resisting change. And they have to swing those tools with persistence. Leaders rely more on their sense of persistence than on their talent or their education as President Calvin Coolidge observed:

> *"Nothing in this world can take the place of persistence. Talent will not. Nothing is more common than unsuccessful men with great talent.*
>
> *Genius will not. Unrewarded genius is almost a proverb. Education will not. The world is full of educated derelicts. Persistence and determination alone are omnipotent."*

The image of a stone cutter at work drives home the significance of continuing to persist even in the absence of any feedback. "Have you ever watched a stone cutter at work," asked Benjamin Disraeli, the former British statesman? "He will hammer away at rock for perhaps 100 times without a crack showing in it. Then at the 101st blow it will split in two. It is not that blow alone which accomplishes the result but the 100 others that went before it as well." So speak loudly & carry a big sledgehammer. Be willing and able to swing it persistently over and over again to make your point. And then be willing and able to raze the past in order to raise a brighter and stronger future. See *Creation Out of Devastation* on page 71, Mint 27.

Today's ImproveMINT

Embrace change boldly & visually to keep your leadership thinking in mint condition.

●

Mint 78

Analogy:
Turning Huh? Into Aha!

Reading time: 3:24

You're at the most important part of your speech, the part where you are explaining an important policy or process. But something is wrong, terribly wrong. You see the eyes of your audience glaze over. And you can almost hear their collective sigh. They are confused, so confused that they have tuned you out. What do you do? Call in your A-team. A for Analogy. The A-team, properly armed and purposely detailed, will wake up your audience so that they not only hear what you are saying, they will understand it and more significantly know how to apply it. Use an analogy whenever you need to explain a new process or new procedure particularly to a general audience. The dictionary defines analogy as a "similarity in some respects between things that are otherwise dissimilar."

To create an analogy, first define an object with which your audience is already familiar. Then look for characteristics in that object that could be compared to traits or various aspects of the concept or process you are trying to communicate. Let's say you are a nutritionist and you want to deliver a speech for a general audience on the value of fasting. No doubt many in the audience would be less than enthusiastic at the prospect of not eating every 4-5 hours. In summoning up your A-team, you begin your speech first with an analogy, something with which the audience is already familiar, something that engages the audience and builds greater understanding. In conducting your research on fasting you found that one of the key benefits to fasting is that your digestive system gets a lot more efficient after a fast. During a fast, the body reorganizes parts and pieces of the digestive system that normally are too busy digesting food and in the process the digestive system repairs and/or resets various functions to become even more efficient. Is there something in your audience's everyday lives that reorganizes itself and gets more efficient especially when you are NOT using that process as you normally would? How about computers? Is there any way to connect computer processing to a fasting process that results in a similar outcome: reorganizing the system to make it work better? Consider this analogy of defragging a computer that one leader used to open a speech on fasting to a general audience.

"Fasting to the human body is like the defragging process to a computer. It forces your system to take a rest so that it can reset, restore and repair itself. And then run a lot more efficiently.

"When you fast, you stop eating for several days and free up 60 percent of the body's energy that the digestive system regularly uses. Working at only 40 percent its usual processing speed, your digestive system redirects its excess energy to reset, restore and repair itself to be that much more effective and efficient when eating resumes.

"Likewise a computer consumes a lot of energy looking for various files that get spread out in your system. When you defrag your computer you help the computer more efficiently digest its files."

Indeed, creating analogies like that - turning huh? into aha!—is a key leadership skill. Tom Peters writes in his book *Thriving on Chaos*: "An essential factor in leadership is the capacity to influence and organize meaning for members of the organization." With your A-team.

Today's ImproveMINT

***Use analogy to explain complex issues
to keep your leadership thinking in mint condition.***

●

Mint 79

Savoring Your M&Ms: Magical Metaphors

Reading time: 3:23

Who wants to be a Designated Driver? Not many hands went up in the college dorm. But then a leader in the group reframed the question: Who wants to become the <u>Life of the Party</u>? Now that role immediately had more takers. Meanwhile in another college dorm, science students were discussing the merits of various career opportunities. The subject turned to astronomy. No one in the group was too star-gazed over the prospective of spending their careers looking through telescopes. But then a leader in the group reframed the question: Who wants to become a <u>Peeping Tom at the Keyhole of Eternity</u> as author Arthur Koestler called astronomers. Metaphors can trigger a creative perspective that turns a negative into a positive. Consider:

1. Making an appointment with a <u>Smile Stylist</u> instead of a dentist
2. Eating <u>God's Candy</u> instead of fruit
3. Visiting "the <u>Delivery Room for the Birth of Ideas</u>" as author Norman Cousins called the library.

No wonder, designing and utilizing metaphors that more fully explain, engage and enlighten is a valued leadership skill. Metaphors are so powerful that Greek philosopher Aristotle said: "The greatest thing by far is to have mastered the metaphor." And the Spanish philosopher and writer Jose Ortega y Gasset added, "The metaphor is probably the most fertile power possessed by man." Poets certainly have mastered the magic of the metaphor to broaden our perspective. For example Henry Wadsworth Longfellow metaphorically connected a grave to the concept of a bridge *("The grave itself is but a covered bridge leading from light to light through a brief darkness.")* Activists know the magic of the metaphor: Strategic Defense Initiative (SDI) to some became Star Wars to others. Metaphors provide new meaning on an old idea. For example: Do you throw gum in a trash can or deposit it into a <u>Gum Bank</u> as the sign at the roller skating rink encourages? Do you purchase window accessories —curtain rods, rings, tie-backs and swag holders—or do you purchase <u>Jewelry for Your Windows</u>? And do your employees work in small cramped offices or in a <u>Cocoon</u> as Charles Lindbergh called his cockpit?

The dictionary defines a metaphor as an implied comparison between two unlike things that have something significant in common. Here's how a pastor compared his work life to a variety of birds and ended up with a bonus paycheck.

> **"People expect the clergy to have the grace of a swan, the friendliness of a sparrow, the strength of an eagle and the night hours of an owl. And some people expect such a bird to live on the food of a canary."**

And in 1886, Kodak compared the technology of its new camera to a "mirror with a memory." Kodak connected two dissimilar things that have something in common. A camera's film is the memory and the lens is the mirror. Link the two "knowns" to the unknown —a camera—and a metaphor is born. Savor your M&Ms, your Magical Metaphors to better digest your leadership initiatives.

Today's ImproveMINT

Master the magic of the metaphor
to keep your leadership thinking in mint condition.

●

Mint 80

Searching
For The Beauty Within

Reading time: 3:35

Forlorn and frustrated, the prostitute was mired in the mud of her past. So devastated she convinced herself that she "was born in a pile of horse manure" and that she would "die in a pile of horse manure." Yet he saw something more enriching and ennobling in her eyes, something more promising in her future. To him she was not a prostitute, she was The Sweet One. She grimaced whenever he called her The Sweet One. She could never live up to that sweet expectation. No way, she protested. But he persisted. He was convinced she was The Sweet One. The more he persisted over time, the less she protested over time. And then slowly but steadily the more confident she became in living up to that Sweet One appellation and ensuing reputation.

That's why the most effective leaders design and develop nicknames as a tool to mine the exemplary performance they know is buried deep in some of their errant employees. In fact, nicknames — rooted in an act of faith— can inspire a change in behavior that surprises and delights. The Sweet One (Dulcinea) for example in the Broadway musical play and later film: *The Man From La Mancha*, began doing works of compassion for others. The play ends with the former prostitute personally affirming her new identity: "My name is Dulcinea" when someone calls her by her real name Aldonza. As a leader, how do you become a Don Quixote expressing that kind of act of faith in others? How do you engineer a deep seated trust in others that can transform behavior and renew a tattered reputation. How do you anoint key individuals on your staff with meaningful nicknames that positively impact their performance and your bottom line? How do you cultivate the hidden Dulcinea's on your staff—those staffers known only superficially and often for something less than perfect performance in their past?

Here's how: First take your time. Study your staff carefully over time rather than simply react to their current behavior. And when you study them, take a lesson from Johnny Depp's lead character in the movie *Don Juan DeMarco:* Don't be LIMITED by your eyesight. Look at individuals on your staff more strategically than ever before with a feeling, with an intuitive sense that goes deeper than assessing their past performance. Look more widely, more comprehensively, more astutely than merely with your eyes. Search out the "beauty" within. In the movie, *Don Juan DeMarco*, Depp's character tells his psychiatrist— played by Marlon Brando— that his alluring influence over women stems from their "sense that I search out their beauty that is within them until it overwhelms everything else. And then they cannot avoid that desire to release that beauty and envelop me in it."

Forget the sexual overtones or the Hollywood hype and sexist script that only an actor like Depp could get away with on the silver screen. The key point is to focus on POSITIVE behaviors. Look for the possibilities—the potential —in a staff member whose performance levels have fallen. Rely on your insight more than your sight and search "for the beauty within" as Don Juan DeMarco asserts. Indeed, leadership is an act of faith that brings out the best in others. Leaders infuse others with a greater sense of purpose, dignity and worth. Leaders breathe life into others. They inspire from the Latin *inspirare* "to breathe." See *Parlay Your Pygmalion Power* on page 134, Mint 50.

Today's ImproveMINT

Generate positive nicknames
to keep your leadership thinking in mint condition.

●

Mint 81

Public Speaking In a Bathrobe & Beyond

Reading time: 3:08

Mandatory meeting at 7 a.m. on a Sunday! Are you kidding me? That was the prevailing reaction when the president called an unprecedented meeting of all 600 managers in his company one Sunday morning—the last day of a three-day conference at a resort. Everyone grumbled getting up that early because of a venue scheduling conflict. At 6:59 a.m. the huge hotel ballroom was filled. But the president looked like a no-show. Finally at exactly 7 a.m. the president walked on stage. In his bathrobe! Waving a cup of coffee in his hand, he said: "Geez, who scheduled this early morning meeting anyway?" The crowd laughed. They howled even louder when the president disrobed, revealing his suit coat and tie. Fully dressed in his business attire, he approached the lectern. Finally when the laughter died down, the audience was fully awake and ready to listen and learn.

The bathrobe-disrobing president tapped into what his audience was feeling at that moment. He connected with them, personally. He demonstrated his emotional intelligence. And they were now more attentive to his message even at 7 in the morning on a normal day off for most employees. You might not see yourself ever making a spectacle out of yourself on stage like that in front of your employees, but maybe one of these following attention-getting scenarios may spark your creative thinking to first capture the attention of an audience before you try to deliver your message:

1. **A vice president** threw some coins on the table. She asked for someone in the audience to tell her how much money was on the table. The audience

member counted it. "87 cents," he said. "Yes, that is the face value but now examine the coins more closely and you will see they are dated 1924. That makes them worth $1,078 not 87 cents. We too are sitting on a treasure chest of valuable information, more valuable than we see at face value."

2. **A department head** began swinging away at a piñata with a baseball bat. After the cascade of candy flooded the floor, he said: "I feel a little like this piñata. Everybody seems to be hitting me up for more resources. I feel battered. Our resources are depleting."

3. **The division president** began speaking in French to her English-speaking audience. She stopped suddenly and said in fluent English: "No wonder our customers are confused. No wonder our sales are down. We're not speaking the customer's language."

The most effective leaders stage their presentations with much more than words. They know they first have to connect with their audience visually, personally and purposefully. Even at 7 on a Sunday morning. In a bathrobe.

Today's ImproveMINT

Visually connect with your audience
BEFORE speaking
to keep your leadership thinking
in mint condition.

Mint 82

Flash Your Lt. Columbo Badge of Confusion

Reading time: 3:45

After delivering his speech with authority and conviction, the vice president was surprised at the less than enthusiastic applause from his audience. Then a colleague whispered to him as they left the auditorium together that his speech may have been more warmly received if he had spoken more like Lt. Columbo than Sgt. Joe Friday. TV fans of yesteryear will recall Lieutenant Columbo, the disheveled and somewhat disoriented detective that actor Peter Falk made famous in *Columbo*, the network television series. Lieutenant Columbo was the polar opposite of the stern, button-downed, highly disciplined, no-nonsense, just-the-facts-man Sgt. Friday— the detective that Jack Webb made famous in the network television series *Dragnet*.

The vice president realized too late that being efficient—i.e. professional—is necessary but never sufficient in leading others particularly from the podium. Sure you have to have your facts but the most influential speakers don't let their facts have them. They vet them with third-party objectivity from authentic sources. Then they breathe life into their facts and personality into their figures so they don't come across as a robotic, mono-toned know-it-all. In fact, behavioral research shows that an audience is more likely to be persuaded by someone less polished, someone more prone to mistakes, someone just like them —warts and all. After all, the most effective leaders know the bromide is correct: *"No one cares how much you know until they know how much you care."* Lt. Columbo cared about the victims in his crime investigations. He camouflaged his caring modus operandi and cunning investigative mind with his personal eccentricities—from wearing a wrinkled trench coat to driving a junker of a car. And despite his awkward interactions and haphazard interruptions ('just one more thing") he consistently outsmarted the rich, intelligent and sophisticated murderers every week on national television. His bumbling behavior invariably influenced others to let down their guard and more readily accept new information or verify old information that helped him solve the crime at the expense of his better dressed adversaries.

Lt. Columbo demonstrated a key leadership behavior: be more authentic not simply authoritative. Be real—not just a big deal. Beware of hiding behind your title, your pedigree, your degree, or your decree. And double down on your *dubitatio*. Rhetoricians define *dubitatio* as a personal form of *aporia* which is doubt or ignorance—feigned or real—used as a rhetorical device to make the speaker seem more human, more real and ultimately more honest. With *dubitatio* you lower audience expectations so that the speaker (or detective) can surprisingly wow 'em in the end. That's what Abraham Lincoln did at his Coopers Union speech in part to win the White House. Historians noted Lincoln's "rumpled appearance" after his 4-day, 3-night journey to New York City on five different trains. Some in the audience seemed to smirk at his high-pitched voice and besmirch his "gangly rough-hewn western" looks. Yet Lincoln's words were so well-researched, his thoughts so elegantly woven together that the newspapers the next day hailed Lincoln's candidacy for president of the United States. Lt. Columbo would have been proud of his fellow Wrinkled Warrior wearing his coat-of-arms—showcasing his values and vision virtually on his sleeve—with such professional distinction and disciplined emotional intelligence.

Today's ImproveMINT

Beware of looking too slick, too polished
to keep your leadership thinking in mint condition.

Mint 83

Take Your Audience For a Joy Ride

Reading time: 3:29

Next time you step on to a podium or up to a lectern think of yourself climbing into the driver's seat. Now take your audience for a joy ride as you deliver your speech. Remember your first joy ride? The fun is in the acceleration not just the velocity. Accelerate to exhilarate The exhilaration is in the dynamics—zooming up and down hills. So too in effective public speaking where dynamic leaders exercise their dynamics of speech: speeding up and slow down, shifting gears and varying their pitch—the whine of their engines. Leading speakers vary their tone, from a screaming exhaust to a whisper of the brakes. Yet too often public speakers take the joy out of their joy ride with an emphasis on one extreme or the other: too fast or too slow. We hear overly excited leaders with their foot slammed down on the accelerator screaming with the passion of a preacher seemingly for miles on end. Too much. Or we hear leaders riding the brake, unsure of where they're heading—doling out fact after fact, drip by drip, in a tepid monotone. Too slow. Pace yourself.

The most effective leaders realize that pacing is the key to effective speech delivery—assuming the content is tailored to the audience's interests, concerns and needs. To help you remember the importance of pacing, envision a roller coaster. Now, take your audience for a thrilling, breath-taking, memorable and enjoyable joy ride. Leverage the suspenseful build up —s-l-o-w-l-y point by point by point—just like the roller coaster clicks along the tracks as it inches its way so slowly, so methodically up that first incline and then halts briefly at the top to heighten the interest and build a sense of urgency in their message before roaring down. The most effective leaders also use the pacing technique to better govern their volume to attract and retain more listeners. An effective leader can command attention with a soft sound that builds over time—getting louder and LOUDER—much like *Bolero*, the classic composed by Maurice Ravel as a single melody repeated that gets progressively louder with each rendition. Couple that stentorian voice with its opposite—SILENCE—and you'll command the attention of your audience in stunning style. The silence rendered during a pregnant pause can be deafening. Periodic pauses pack a punch. Even a whisper can command the attention of the restless audience. No wonder Oliver Wendell Holmes cited the consummate skill leaders exhibit in delivering the pregnant pause from the podium:

> *"Talking is like playing on a harp. There is as much laying the hands on the strings to stop the vibrations as in twanging them to bring out their music."*

Silence can startle. Stopping the vibrations can ironically have a vibrating affect and a memorable effect. The most effective leaders learn how to sneak up on the audience with a pregnant pause the way composer Joseph Haydn does in Symphony No. 94. In the 16th measure of the second movement, there is a single loud chord and then: Silence. The surprising restart of the music is so stunning this symphony is known as *The Surprise Symphony*. The leadership lesson is clear: Surprise your audience with vocal variety. Surprise your audience with a dynamic joy ride they will feel for a long time and remember even longer to more fully understand, apply and act on your message.

Today's ImproveMINT:

Vary your pace in speaking publicly
to keep your leadership thinking in mint condition.

●

Mint 84

Taking the Scum
Off Your Mind

Reading time: 3:04

S tabbing her long thin spoon into the mountain of ice cream, the four-year-old tasted the hot fudge, pursed her lips and grimaced: "Oh, that's hot." Then she swallowed and tasted the ice cream. "Oh, that's cold!" Hot fudge sundaes are hot and cold at the same time. They're a composite of opposites. So are leaders. After all, the most effective leaders are exemplars of opposites. They're loners who are never really alone. They readily accept the paradox of life around them where those in the know know a curve is really a series of straight lines. No wonder former Chief Justice Oliver Wendell Holmes, Jr. once observed:

"There's nothing like a
paradox to take
the scum off your mind."

Parlaying the paradox is a leader's modus operandi. Leaders juggle contradictions and dilemmas with finesse. Leaders celebrate counter-intuitiveness anywhere and everywhere: from the carpenter using something rough (sandpaper) to make something smooth to the fire fighter conquering a forest fire in part by starting another fire (a fire wall). As a paradox-appreciating leader, you find yourself working in "exciting serenity" as artist Paul Cezanne once characterized his working style. You learn to be "quick but never in a hurry" as former UCLA basketball coach John Wooden exhorted his players. And you learn to get up even when you can't as boxing champion Jack Dempsey paradoxically defined a champion. To help you take the scum off your mind and keep your leadership thinking in mint condition, consider the following Paean to the Paradox:

To Know is Not to Know

The more they know the more they don't know or as Albert Einstein noted: "As the sphere of light increases so does the darkness surrounding it."

To Be Certain is to be Uncertain

"We are often most in the dark when we are the most certain and the most enlightened when we are the most confused," writes M. Scott Peck in his book *The Road Less Traveled.*

Stay Apart to Stay Together

Poet Kahlil Gibran notes that the roof of a temple is strong because its pillars are far apart.

To Build It Up, Break it Down

To make paper stronger, you beat it. And to make copper stronger you hammer it.

Let those paradoxes wash away some of the scum off your mind so that you can lead more creatively. And maybe even LICK your competition with the same personal satisfaction as enjoying an ice cream sundae. Hot and cold.

Today's ImproveMINT

Parlay the power of the paradox
to keep your leadership thinking in mint condition.

●

Mint 85

Kiss My Atlas!

Reading time: 3:51

K iss my Atlas! The sarcastic words screamed throughout the scorned community of Yuba City, CA after Rand McNally (Atlas) ranked it the worst livable city in the United States. Yuba City residents were so infuriated they defiantly wore *Kiss My Atlas* T-shirts and burned copies of the Atlas in bonfire bonanzas. Their *Kiss My Atlas* T-shirts illustrated the power of the visual medium in the delivery of a meaningful and memorable message. Their *Kiss My Atlas* T-shirts also demonstrated what most effective leaders already know: be visual. Show more than tell. Audiences see a message long before they hear it, according to the research of Albert Mehrabian at the University of California at Los Angeles (UCLA). Professor Mehrabian found that:

- 55 % of information is received visually.
- 38% is communicated in the tone of voice
- 7% of information is dependent on the words

That's why the most successful leaders orchestrate their message visually. George Steinbrenner, then the owner of the New York Yankees, dressed like Napoleon atop a horse for a *Sports Illustrated* cover photo to mark his return from exile to professional baseball. A *Time* cover story on the inventor of the geodesic dome depicted the head of Buckminster Fuller formed as a geodesic dome. And in pre-American Revolutionary War days, Ben Franklin's newspaper in Pennsylvania pictured the image of a snake, cut in eight different sections. The headline screamed with little subtlety: "Join or Die." Headlines can also beam with a light touch of humor that generates wide smiles and long miles down memory lane in retaining audience attention and message memorability. Consider this headline on a favorite T-shirt of science teachers. Two atoms are talking to each other. One says "I've lost an electron." The other responds: "Are you positive?"

Here are a few more meaningful and attention-catching headlines calling out creative ideas that will spark your visual leadership thinking:

1. An orthodontist issues a ticket—*Admit One This Date Only* — as a confirmation of an appointment, and leverages teenagers' penchant for attending fun events (movies, concerts, sports events) with a ticket.   .

2. A leader of diversity at a large corporation has a jar full of multi-colored, multi-flavored jelly beans as the centerpiece for the conference table in her office.

3. And a mortgage officer's business card pictures a masked man on a white horse. The mortgage officer's title on the card is *The Loan Ranger*. It's a reference to the *Lone Ranger* of radio and TV fame- a former Texas Ranger who fought injustice and helped people in distress even though he wore a black mask. On radio and TV, no one could forget the Lone Ranger. And it real life few will forget they met The Loan Ranger.

Today's ImproveMINT

*Use visual language to keep
your leadership thinking in mint condition.*

●

Mint 86

Interruptions: The Spice of Life

Reading time: 3:39

Whewwwwww! I'm snoring on the couch while the television set is blaring. The louder the television the louder my snoring (or so I am told). Then suddenly, I awake. What happened? Oh, my wife just turned off the television. Why is it that you can sleep through the blaring noise of the television set but you awake when someone finally grants you the silence that should have kept you in dreamland? Could there be a leadership learning in that unwanted awakening experience? Maybe. At least that awakening experience helped me better understand and value the dynamics of change that fuels every leader's agenda. Maybe this idea will help you too leverage change even more effectively.

The Flashlight Theory of Change

Consider: The *Flashlight Theory of Change*. What if you thought of interruptions as so many flashes of light that spice your performance? After all, it's the periodic FLASH of the light that brightens and enlightens our lives to get ahead—not the consistent light of a flashlight beaming a steady light ahead. To better cope with change, think of your television as if it were the beam of a flashlight, a beam of light that can literally put you to sleep. Bathed in that beam of a flashlight consistently over time, you can become so accustomed to the bright lights and blaring sound that you fall asleep no matter how funny Jimmy Fallon's monolog. But you quickly awaken when that flashlight is turned off. That interruption in the status quo invigorates your sense of anticipation and renewal. So think of change as an interruption in the status quo, an interruption that spices your performance with a vim and vigor; an interruption—a flash of light—that regenerates, renovates, and rejuvenates.

CHANGE REGENERATES: More than 98 percent of all atoms in the human body are replaced – changed—in less than one year, says Dr. Deepak Chopra in his book *Ageless Body, Timeless Mind.* In fact, humans change their outer skin completely every 27 days. **CHANGE RENOVATES**: Farmers nourish their land with change. They rotate their crops. The soil needs to be refreshed with new nutrients. Likewise tree farmers nourish their land with change. They clear their land every 40 years to give birth to new trees. **CHANGE REJUVENATES**: Nathaniel Hawthorne, the author, once observed: "Human nature will not flourish if is planted and replanted in the same worn out soil."

Indeed life itself would not flourish if human beings weren't literally replanted (buried) in the wake of the ultimate interruption: death. Without death—without the ultimate change in life—life would have no meaning, no beginning, no ending and ultimately no spice. But with death comes change that spices life, that interrupts the status quo, that awakens the leader in each of us to a new beginning—a new beginning that reaffirms your value and vision, your potential and purpose, and your discipline and direction.

The leadership lesson is clear: Think of interruptions as so many spices of life. Then turn on your <u>Flashlight Theory of Change</u> and awaken your full potential. No matter if you do snore at times in front of Jimmy Fallon et al. Whewwwwww!

Today's ImproveMINT

***Appreciate the value of change
to keep your leadership thinking in mint condition.***

Mint 87

Churning Your
Spilled Milk

Reading time: 3:29

Revisions. "I love revisions," says novelist Katherine Paterson, "where else in life can spilled milk be transformed into ice cream?" No wonder that churning your spilled milk into ice cream through careful and thoughtful rewriting, editing and revising — over and over again — is the requisite skill of strategic leaders and cogent speakers. Yet too many executives are too quick to spill the milk of their ideas—their knowledge, experience and expertise right now rather than churn that milk into an ice cream of thought and insight over time. Their Spilled Milk of Ideas (writing) churned into the Ice Cream of Thought (rewriting) become more palatable and portable to the audience. After all, your revised writing and thinking—like frozen ice cream—can be packaged and carried a lot easier than a bottle of milk (writing off the top of your head).

Still too many executives are too ready on the spur of the moment to pour their ideas out of their proverbial milk bottles of expertise and experience. They are like the executive who was asked: How long it would take you to prepare a 10-minute presentation? He said two weeks "but if you want a two-hour presentation I'm ready right now." Too many executives are too quick to regurgitate what they already knew and too reluctant to propagate something new. That's why the most effective leaders embrace revising as part of the writing process, a continuous improvement process based on feedback and self-reflection that turns the prosaic into the poetic. After all, the more a revising-oriented leader moves around the words and thoughts in their first draft, the more the words seem to dance into stirring thoughts. In dancing with their words and phrases, leaders churn their own creative thinking process that moves your message from simply telling to amply compelling. "The best writing is rewriting," noted E.B. White, the co-author of <u>Elements of Style</u> one of the 100 best and most influential books written in the English language (from 1923), according to a 2011 list in TIME Magazine.   In rewriting, leaders engage in "thinking on paper" as author William Zinsser defined writing in his book *On Writing Well.* No wonder research shows that writers of various documents—from speeches to books— revise their writing 4-13 times to churn out new and improved drafts. Edward Everett churned. In writing and rewriting his two-hour speech dedicating the Gettysburg Cemetery, Edward Everett churned eight weeks. Abraham Lincoln churned. In writing and rewriting his three-minute Gettysburg Address, Abraham Lincoln churned three weeks and completed at least six different drafts. And Mario Cuomo churned a total of 16 hours over a 10-day period in writing and revising his 20-minute keynote speech at the 1984 Democratic Convention.

    In rewriting, the most effective leaders give their writing text texture —churning their Spilled Milk of Thought into an ice cream of ideas, experiences and insights that we can savor. Each churn creates a texture that gives greater meaning and depth to their writing, a churning that is generated *a fiortiori* (stronger with evidence) not constructed *a priori* (from an earlier version) as the legal folks say. Each churn of an idea, word, or phrase makes the final thought that much more relevant and that more meaningful to this audience. The leadership lesson is clear: in researching and writing your next speech remember that one good churn deserves another. Thoughtfully.

Today's ImproveMINT

Revise and rewrite often
to keep your leadership thinking in mint condition.

●

Mint 88

Writing a
PreSCRIPTion

Reading time: 3:31

O pening the cover of his prepared text the executive settles in at the podium. Then he abruptly closes his script and declares: "Today I just want to speak to you from my heart." Balderdash! After all, EVERY meaningful and memorable speech is delivered first and foremost "from the heart" or else you lose your audience's attention unless you have the power of the pay check to command their interest. After all, your audience's B-S meters are set too high to keep your voice in their ears— to really listen and learn from your speech—without the power of the pay check.

Yet, executives most often "speak from the heart" and eschew their prepared remarks for self-serving reasons. Some speaker/leaders fear reading a speech makes them look less authoritative. Other speaker/leaders want to be perceived more conversational and less programmed. But the most enlightened speaker/leaders come to realize their script can counter-intuitively help them look more authoritative and conversational.

That's why the most effective speakers learn how to read their speeches with feeling that engages audiences more fully in their message and engenders a more conversational, more intimate tone. The first step in reading your text more persuasively with or without a teleprompter is to first think of your script as a preSCRIPTion. Then you can gain more direct control of the dosage (tone of your speech), the duration (time of your speech) and the direction (strategic intent of your speech). That's why effective preSCRIPTions are too important to be written solely on your heart, too important to be written ONLY on your shirt cuffs (off the cuff) or ONLY on your fingertips (e.g. humorist Mark Twain). Even with a preSCRIPTion, you can develop a more conversational style that accentuates eye contact and personal appeal. But it takes practice like this:

1. Select a key passage in your written text.
2. Read that passage over and over again until you begin to commit the phrasing and thought structure to memory.
3. Mentally record your voice: Think of the process of repeating those key passages out loud to yourself over and over again, as if you were mentally recording your voice during these rehearsals.
4. Then during the delivery of your speech, you hit the "play button" on your mental recorder and target your audience's pain or pleasure more directly. By heart. From the heart.

With your PreSCRIPTion in hand, you memorialize more than simply memorize your thoughts, ideas and memories. You celebrate your memories. You commemorate your memories. You repeat phrases out loud over and over again with empathy. You amplify and sanctify your message with a greater infusion of your humanity. Then with your PreSCRIPTion in hand, you can help your audience feel better, live healthier, work more productively and enjoy life more creatively. As prescribed with no side effects. By heart, sincerely. Not "from the heart" casually.

Today's ImproveMINT

Write a preSCRIPTion for your audience
to keep your leadership thinking in mint condition.

●

Mint 89

Who's Farding
In the Car?

Reading time: 3:24

Farting — not exactly the kind of word you expect to hear on a serious radio talk show. Maybe "farting" is a word you might hear shock jock Howard Stern utter. But certainly not broadcasting baron Rush Limbaugh, who boasts that he performs "with half my brain tied behind my back just to make it fair because I have talent on loan from God." Even God may have winced at this Limbaugh assault on the ears of millions of radio listeners across the country. Many were enraged. Why is the grand master of political talk radio talking about a woman who was arrested for farting in her car? At least that's what they thought they heard him say. Radio station managers around the country started to pull the plug on his show when they heard him respond to the obvious question: how could the police tell she was farting? "Because the police could see it," said Limbaugh, his tongue firmly in his cheek. Then Limbaugh exonerated himself and educated his listeners on the verb "to fard." The dictionary says farding means to put cosmetics on the face. The lady in her car was arrested for putting lipstick on as she drove.

Leaders in the real world can't afford to say SOME thing that their audience hears as ANOTHER thing. That's why the most effective leaders won't subscribe to the arrogance of Humpty Dumpty scornfully telling Alice in Wonderland that: "When I use a word, it means just what I choose it to mean." Not exactly. Word experts tell us that the 500 most common English words have 14,000 different meanings. Consider former newspaper columnist Jack Germond. He meant to say something that others heard very differently no matter how well he enunciated the word designed more to be read than said. Germond ignited a firestorm of outrage on a television program after he criticized black activist Rev. Jesse Jackson for fumbling issues that "went beyond his ken." Many in the television audience heard a racial remark — "skin"— instead of what Germond meant in questioning Jackson's "ken"—his expertise and understanding on the issues.

Yet in showing off their verbal ingenuity leaders have to guard against manipulating others with words the way P.T. Barnum would sucker visitors out of his freak show of a museum with a sign that read: *"This way to Egress."* Patrons were eager to see a new exhibit with a strange sounding name. Of course when they opened the door to enter the Egress "exhibit" they found themselves outside of the museum. Egress is to exit what farding is to putting on makeup—just another more complicated word for the same thing to exploit others. And yet some would-be leaders think using big words adds class to the conversation or status to the individual. The thinking goes that an "environmental home hygienist" should be more well-compensated and respected than a maid and that philatelists, numismatists and plangonologists are smarter than those hobbyists who collect stamps, coins and dolls respectively. Not really.

Leaders know that the use of big words for the sake of big words is a *floccipaucinihilipilification.* That's a mouthful —all 12 syllables and 29 letters of it. And the meaning of this longest word published in the first edition of the Oxford English dictionary is apt. *Floccipaucinihilipilification* means something that is worthless. No matter how polished your ken when you say it. Or how vigorous your farding when you display it.

Today's ImproveMINT

Edit yourself before you speak or write
to keep your leadership thinking in mint condition.

Mint 90

Give Your Problems Their Last Writes

Reading time: 3:01

E xasperating. Two executives are tugging away at a vexing problem. It's getting late in the day and both are frustrated. "What do you think?" says one. "Not sure," responds the other. "Okay, here's a way forward," says the first executive. She reaches into her desk and says: "Take two of these and call me in the morning." Oh, what a headache, both say in unison! "Hey, wait a minute. I'm also going to take two and I'll call YOU in the morning," the other added with a biting sense of humor. The two executives were popping pencils not aspirins. They each wielded two newly-sharpened bright yellow No. 2 pencils. Both executives knew those pencils would do what no aspirin could: help them think.

Writing is Thinking on Paper

After all, "writing is thinking on paper," as author William Zinsser notes in his book *On Writing Well*. The most effective leaders know that writing is a critical thinking skill, a proven method to:

1.   Organize your thoughts.
2.   Establish your point of view.
3.   Pose and defend your argument to make decisions and solve problems.

Indeed, as famed author John Updike observed: "writing is a deeply comforting activity, an ordering and a purging and a bringing into the light what had been hidden an hour before." Richard Nixon, writing in his book *In the Arena*, said: "The process (of writing) forced me to think through all aspects of the problem. It is only when you totally concentrate on a problem that new ideas come to you." In fact novelist William Faulkner the more he wrote the more ideas he had. Faulkner said that he never knew "what I think about something until I read what I've written on it." University of Michigan professor Karl Weick echoed that observation: "I know what I think when I see what I say." And author Paul Rand said his writing developed his sense of understanding like bricks of thought on key design issues that he arranged creatively and the "byproduct" was "a book for other people."

Writing—like mortar—cements the thinking process. In fact, writing is much like building a house, according to author and former Great Britain Prime Minister Winston Churchill: "The technique is different, the materials are different, but the principle is the same. The foundation has to be laid, the data assembled and the premises must bear the weight of the conclusions." And all of that takes a sharp mind and in at least one famous example plenty of sharp pencils. Consider John Steinbeck's Pencil Power. Early in his writing career, the famed author of *The Grapes of Wrath* and *Of Mice and Men* would sharpen 24 pencils every morning before beginnings his thinking on paper. Did the finer points on his pencils help him develop his finer points on paper? He didn't have to say. He let his sharpened pencil speak up for him in creating such memorable characters as Tom Joad in *The Grapes of Wrath* and George Milton and Lennie Small in *Of Mice and Men* and ultimately the more pointed and precise his problem solving (in story and character development). At any rate, the leadership lesson for all of us is clear: Give your problems their last "writes" with a pencil in hand.

Today's ImproveMINT

*Use your writing skill as problem-solving tool
to keep your leadership thinking in mint condition.*

●

Mint 91

The Handshake You Leave Behind

Reading time: 3:18

How well does your business card engage your clients or customers with an attention-getting visual and meaningful and memorable message? How well does it serve as "the handshake you leave behind?" That's how author Lynella Grant (*The Business Card Book*) characterizes the Sensational Seven—the seven square inches of highly coveted and valued marketing real estate on the business card you carry in your purse or wallet. To help you firm up your grip on the printed handshake you leave behind, consider these creative business cards:

1. On the back side of a financial advisor's business card, there are three actual postage stamps:

    *   A 10-cent stamp captioned <u>1975</u>.
    *   A 32-cent stamp captioned <u>1995</u>.
    *   And a 49-cent stamp captioned <u>2015</u>.

    The impact of inflation on your earning power is clearly evident in the price escalation over four decades. Hence the reason why you need a good financial advisor. Subtle yet strategic.

2. You can also use your business card as a discount coupon. On the back side of an auto repair shop's business card it says "We need more customers like you. Please give this card to someone you know and we will give each of you $20 off your next bill." Then there is a line for the name of the person referred and the name of the current customer. Now that tiny

business card from an auto repair shop is like having an extra $20 in your wallet or purse.

3. You can also add value with more customer-centered information on the back side of business card: an insurance company provides 4-steps to making a claim, a church provides the cross streets of a map, and a men's clothing store salesman pens in his weekly work schedule "for your convenience."

Meanwhile other business cards are so well strategically designed that you get a "feeling" about the company just by touching or seeing their business card— long before reading it.

- A woodworking company prints its business card on a sample piece of paper-thin red cedar.
- A window design company features window-like cutouts on its business card.
- A cabinetmaker positions a level tool on the top of the business card and a level tool at the bottom of the card to frame the company name.
- A music therapist's company name is printed over a five-line musical staff.
- Baby-delivery doctors stylize the first letter in their company name to make it look like an umbilical cord.
- A lawn sprinkling company features a green triangle space at the bottom of its business card with a tree growing on the slope.

The leadership lesson is clear: Infuse your business card design with more personality that grips others like the firm handshake you leave behind.

Today's ImproveMINT

Take your business cards personally
to keep your leadership thinking in mint condition.

Mint 92

Saying 'I'm Sorry' the Write Way

Reading time: 3:18

My new boss had my back. "I'll be there to give you moral support," he told me as I prepared for a presentation the next morning at a large sales meeting. It really didn't matter that my boss never showed. After all, he clearly had confidence in me. Besides, the presentation went well as expected. As soon as I got back to the office, my boss stopped me before I even had a chance to sit down. He looked at me and said contritely: "I screwed up. I just forgot all about it. I am sorry. So sorry. That's for you." My boss pointed to an envelope on my desk. The envelope had my name written in perfect penmanship. Inside there was a motivational card that said "Challenge" on the front. I opened the card and read his carefully handwritten apology.

I knew my new boss as a highly successful leader who had brandished his reputation as street-smart, don't-mess-with-me guy for more than 30 years at the same company. That's why I felt goose bumps sprinkle all over my neck as I read his words: "I'm sorry. I screwed up...." Each letter he wrote in his best penmanship seemed so thoughtfully scripted. His expensive fountain pen seemed to ooze drops like so many virtual tears. After reading his apology, I needed to swallow before getting back to work. He could have easily hid behind the managerial code for screwing up: *"I had another emergency that I had to handle right away and couldn't get over to your meeting."* But he didn't. He just simply confessed. He admitted his mistake. My boss's apology—in person and in writing—really touched me and rekindled my commitment to him personally and our company collectively. From that day of the apology going forward, I seemed to bring my "A" game to the office much more often. I felt like I was more productive. Maybe I was just working longer rather than smarter. Not sure. But I figured if my new boss cared that much about me, I should care even more about making him look good in hiring me in the first place.

My new boss-turned-pen-pal taught me a significant leadership lesson that day. It's a lesson that has served me well in developing teams and building trust over the years. Value the dignity and worth of your staff. Be true to your word, especially if you are vowing support – materially, physically or spiritually. And if that bond of trust is broken, be quick, vocal, and verbal in apologizing personally and documenting your apology with your signature statement. It's one thing to perfunctorily mouth the words —"I'm sorry"—and call it good. It's another thing to sit down, swallow your pride and your positional authority. Then take the time to search for a Hallmark Helper (inspirational cards, write out your apology and personally deliver it. That Pen-Pal approach takes enormous emotional intelligence backed with a well-executed plan of caring. No click does the trick. No hiding behind E-mail.

After all, the ability to write is uniquely human and the act of writing in your longhand is particularly personal. Later, I found out that my new boss stocked inspirational blank greeting cards in his office the way others stock business cards. Chances are pretty good that I was not the first—nor the last of his direct reports— to be "carded."

Today's ImproveMINT

Apologize in writing and in person
to keep your leadership thinking in mint condition.

●

Mint 93

Catching the 5:15
Train of Thought

Reading time: 2:57

Weekend yeeehah! It's 5:15 on a Friday afternoon. Do you know where your staff is? Of course not. Not in a digital, work anywhere, anytime, anyhow world. Yet the most effective leaders always know where their staffs are COMING FROM on or about 5:15 pm on a Friday. That's because they were catching the 5:15 Express Train of Thought. The 5:15 is an e-mail that each staff member sends to the team leader by the end of business on Friday. Ideally, this e-mail update—more timely and targeted than a status report—is designed to take only 5 minutes to READ and 15 minutes to WRITE. *The 5:15 should be* pithy and pointed and strategically insightful to the team leader who can then use the information—from customer concerns to competitive gossip heard on the street—to better prepare for his or her staff meeting the following Monday.

In addition to the usual content in a status report—key wins and losses, operational glitches and expected challenges the following week—the 5:15 also asks each staff member to grade their own morale and suggest how the company could improve. "The nice thing is that I can pick up trends or problems quickly," said one leader. "I can forward these notes to the proper people to solve problems or capitalize on opportunities." In addition, the assignment itself of having to catch the 5:15 Express Train of Thought every Friday forces each staff member to be more vigilant throughout the week not only in really listening to customers but also documenting their concerns and stimulating follow-up the following week. The 5:15 also forces staff members to think deliberately about what they did personally the past five days to make the company more successful. Andy Grove, then the CEO at Intel, saw this kind of ad hoc personal communications as a beneficial mental exercise. "Writing a report is important. Reading it often is not," Grove observed. That's because writing per se forces you to focus. The process alone is worthwhile regardless of readership echoes Seth Godin, author of *Linchpin*. He encourages blogging but observes that it doesn't matter if anyone reads your writing. "What matters is the meta condition of thinking about what you are going to say."

Write On! Especially at 5:15 on a Friday afternoon.

After all, the power of the written word is to "organize experience "observed famed author James Michener who wrote more than 40 books including his Pulitzer Prize winning *Tales of the South Pacific.* Writing galvanizes a leader's thinking, clarifies his or her purpose, and seeks to rectify any misunderstandings. Indeed, the process of writing for 15 minutes on what you did the previous week to make the company successful, what problems you encountered and solved, what snafus you corrected reaffirms the value of the employee to himself or herself as well as to the company. No wonder that then Chrysler Chairman Lee Iacocca wrote in his autobiography "the discipline of writing something down is the first step toward making it happen."

Even at 5:15 on a Friday afternoon.

Today's ImproveMINT

Write a 5:15 status update every Friday afternoon to keep your leadership thinking in mint condition.

●

Mint 94

It's Showtime &
You're the Emcee

Reading time: 3:15

Master of Ceremonies. Think of yourself as an emcee—the master of ceremonies—the next time you head a staff meeting. In that role, you will more fully engage your audience with a well thought-out agenda based on a central theme and a coherent purpose. As the emcee you become the FOCAL point but not the focus. You turn the spotlight on everyone else, much like the emcee of a variety show. In fact, the variety show is an appropriate model for today's corporations. Variety is everywhere. Corporations are adding new acts (products) appealing to new audiences (customers) more quickly than ever before. Corporations have fewer people wearing many more different hats. And production is often done with an ensemble of specifically-talented and credentialed performers brought together expeditiously for this one project—on deadline.

As the team leader, you step into Ed Sullivan 's emcee shoes in much the way the television pioneer and famed variety show business leader brought together a variety of performers—from the *Beatles* to *Topo Gigio*—for a weekly project that had to be different and exciting every Sunday night in front of a national television audience. No wonder leaders have become more like emcees than orchestra conductors. Leaders have to do much more than direct others. Leaders have to also set the stage for their followers—their performers, their employees. Leaders have to help them understand and embrace the significance and value of their particular role in the show. And leaders have to be agile and action-oriented to doing it all again next week—differently. Nowhere is the leader's role changing so quickly as in emceeing rather than conducting the regular department or staff meeting. Gone are the days when the leader would simply corral everyone into a meeting room to go through his or her in-basket or to have each person report on what's been happening in their areas. No longer is there a need for department meetings to gurgle like the fountain of information to quench the thirsts of people who need to know. People already know. They are saturated with the flood of information in a 24/7 world. Now they need interpretation, more context—not more content.

So the department meeting now becomes a stage for the "really big show" as Ed Sullivan would say where the emcee—the   team   leader—helps   the   performers (employees)   better   interpret   and   appreciate   the information they have already collected and better connect that information to the interests and concerns of the audience (customers). The leader—as the emcee—sees the meeting room as Ed Sullivan saw the stage. Like a variety show your staff meeting is an opportunity to fill an even more vital relationship-building role where you evolve from a Master of Ceremonies into an emcee of another kind— into a Master Connector who:

1. Makes   the   connection   with   the   performers (employees) more meaningful.
2. Makes   the   connection   between   the   show (company) and the audience (customers) more memorable.
3. Makes   the   total   quality   experience   engaging, entertaining , meaningful and memorable.

Indeed, the "really really really big shew" in Ed Sullivan parlance is all yours -- as long as you make the connections and lead the applause as master of ceremonies.

Today's ImproveMINT

Master the role of master of ceremonies
to keep your leadership thinking in mint condition.

Mint 95

Passionate Introductions Enliven Meetings

Reading time: 4:07

Many meetings seem to end before they begin— in sheer confusion, frustration and exasperation. "A waste of my time," attendees grouse. And no wonder. The meeting agenda skipped the "Coming Attractions." That's why the most compelling leaders invest a little passion and energy into enthusiastically introducing their meeting's featured presenter. They trumpet a little fanfare for the common man (and woman) at their meetings. They herald their meeting magic with a musical flair, much like "*Hail to the Chief*" commands the audience attention at the entrance of the President of the United States.

However too many meetings open with a perfunctory statement of purpose and continue with the important — but impotent—process of handing off the proverbial baton "okay now let me turn the meeting over to…."   No, no, no. That's boring and exasperating to both presenter and the audience especially when neither have the patience to cope with the others' smirks, ridicule and sometimes outright antipathy for the subject matter at hand.   But it doesn't have to be that way. You can thaw the cold stares and maybe even have a little fun at your next meeting. Imagine the two polarized sides in the following meeting scenario: The audience consisted of 18-19 year old college freshmen, tough guys used to being lauded in the press and courted for college football scholarships. The presenter had no direct connection with the audience until the meeting leader ballyhooed the connection. "Gentlemen," beamed the leader of a major college football team during a team meeting, "you are now going to hear about the greatest college fight song from the greatest band director in the history of college football." Hyperbole aside, this team leader and meeting emcee got his audience's undivided attention with a showmanship flair that whetted their appetites to savor the next item on the meeting menu with high expectations. Here's how Bo Schembechler, then the head football coach at the University of Michigan, described this meeting in his book *Bo's Lasting Lessons—The Legendary Coach Teaches the Timeless Fundamentals of Leadership:* "Now I'm sure the freshmen were thinking: What the hell is this? But when (University of Michigan Band Director Dr. William D.) Revelli marched up to the front of that room, he commanded those football players exactly the way he commanded his band. In about five seconds, he had those big lugs in his back pocket!

And the band director waved his arms and the lyrics flowed vigorously from his lips and poignantly from his heart. The coach had invited the band director—n full uniform— to teach the freshmen football players how to sing the Michigan Fight Song. "God he was beautiful," Schembechler recalls of the UM band director. "He didn't just teach them *The Victors.* He taught them Michigan tradition." That tradition REQUIRED a fitting introduction, an introduction that pre-sold and complemented the message, an introduction of a fully uniformed marching band leader paying off on that introduction with a passionate performance that made that meeting more meaningful and memorable. The leadership lesson is clear: The next time you're leading a meeting, find a way to sound your proverbial trumpets in introducing your next featured meeting presenter. Or at least ring the proverbial church bells before your next meeting. HOORAH!

Today's ImproveMINT

Introduce meeting presenters with some fanfare
to keep your leadership thinking in mint condition.

●

Mint 96

Making Your Meetings Snap, Crackle & POP

Reading time: 5:56

Do your meetings—Snap, Crackle and POP—with collaborative thinking and unbridled enthusiasm? Are you smirking right now at the notion of every meeting you attend ACTUALLY being worth your time and attention? Then come with me ye Meeting Martyr. Let's leave Yawn City behind. Let's journey together to Magnificent Meeting Land. Let's explore a Meeting Land where participants stay alert and engaged, where meetings POP with more than an agenda and where each meeting is well anchored, well-defined, and well-positioned:

1.   Well-anchored with a *Premise*
2.   Well-defined with an *Outcome* and
3.   Well-positioned with a *Purpose*

Or POP for short. Sounds too good to be true? After all most meeting planners do an adequate job of defining the purpose of the meeting with a traditional agenda. But only the most effective leaders cogently capture the *Premise* of a meeting for its participants. And the *Premise* is what makes the meeting POP! Think of the *Premise* of your meeting as a bridge—a bridge between the personal values of each meeting participant and the goals of the organization as expressed through the meeting's purpose and desired outcome. If the *Premise* is correct, the Purpose and Outcomes will be more readily achieved. The Premise is the framework for the meeting to take place in the first place. The *Premise* is based on three criteria: Each invited participant has a vested interest in the outcome of the meeting. Each invited participant brings a unique value or perspective that is congruent with the values or perspectives of the organization. Each invited participant can make a difference in the meeting that will impact them personally and professionally. Before calling a meeting, create and distribute a Meeting POP on the Premise/Outcome/Purpose like this:

PREMISE:	Profitability
OUTCOME:	A priority list of programs.
PURPOSE:	To trim the budget by 10%

The *Premise*—profitability—clearly establishes the bridge between the personal values of each meeting participant and the goal of the organization. The Outcome— a priority list of programs—encourages the attendees to come prepared with valid business profit and loss business rationale for continuing to fund their programs. But too many meetings focus primarily on the purpose — to trim the budget. And then too many leaders get defensive and protective of their programs, their budgets, and their power.

However with a well-anchored *Premise* that appeals to everyone's self-interest, even the budget axe may not be as feared. Consider this three-step approach to conducting effective meetings with a POP: Instead of opening the meeting with the perfunctory Statement of Purpose : "We are here to cut our budget by 10%," cite the meeting's *Premise:* "We are here help our company be even more profitable so that we continue to get those salary increases that we all deserve to ease the stress in all our lives and etc." Then cite the desired Outcome (prioritize projects). And only after citing the *Premise* and the Outcome, cite the Purpose (to cut the budget.) This *Premise*-first concept followed by desired OUTCOMES snaps attendees to attention more so than the usual purpose—first meeting opener. And with that snap of attention comes the crackle of new ideas that POP your meeting to life with a sustaining synergy and a rejuvenated energy. Notice the anchoring value in the Why-What-How construction of the _Premise_ Outcome and Purpose of a meeting:

- **WHY:** When you focus first on the WHY of the meeting —on the Premise—the meeting is less threatening and potentially more engaging.
- **WHAT:** Then when you focus on the WHAT of the meeting—on the _Outcome_—the meeting establishes a more focused problem-solving tone to cope with on-going change.
- **HOW:** And then when you focus on the HOW of the meeting—on the _Purpose_—then the Meeting Pre-Reads become more meaningful and relevant.

And your more focused Meeting POP informs your meeting agenda more productively so that you can actually get something done in a meeting! The most effective leaders distribute their POP at least five business days before the meeting to give participants enough pre-read time. Notice in the sample Meeting POP on the next page how the _Premise_ is targeted directly to the concerns of the attendees who have a vested interest and are more apt to make a PERSONAL commitment to the Outcome.

See Sample Meeting POP next page.

Today's ImproveMINT

Cite the Premise of a meeting
to keep your leadership thinking in mint condition.

Meeting POP!
5-minute Leadership Mints Break

WHEN   Friday, October 23 at 10 am as part of our
                  regular staff meeting
WHERE   Department Conference Room

PREMISE

As employees we all deserve professional development opportunities. Yet all of us are too busy to take as much time as we might like to attend leadership development workshops and seminars or attend national professional association conventions to recharge our batteries on a regular basis.

OUTCOME

Create an efficient, on-going, weekly leadership development program for all busy employees that is sensitive to the time constraints and yet reinforces the primary role of a leader to develop other leaders.

PURPOSE

Integrate a 5-minute Leadership Mints Break into our regular staff meetings for all busy employees to enhance their professional and leadership development.

PRE-READ

Be prepared to discuss the concept of the 5-minute Leadership Mints Break as detailed in the newly published book *Leadership Mints*, *101 Ways to Freshen Your Feeling For Leading.* Read Introduction, pages 11-15 and Mint 1, pages 17-18. Get your free copy of *Leadership Mints* by Friday Oct. 16 from (name of person on staff). Thank you in advance for bringing your copy of *Leadership Mints* to the meeting.

Mint 97

Blessing The Team's Inner Sanctum

Reading time: 3:02

F rantically, the little girl climbs into her mother's seat in the movie theater, screaming: "Mommy, Mommy, hold me. I'm scared." A ghost had just careened across the screen in a coming attractions trailer. The little girl gasps at the scene from a horror movie. Her mother comforts her. Sniffling and rubbing her eyes, the little girl blurts: "I don't mind the scary stuff on TV at home because I can put a blanket over my head." Effective leaders always have that proverbial blanket on hand to block out any distractions. They preserve and protect a secure and safe environment for their staffs to work more creatively and comfortably despite the occasional "scary stuff." The most effective leaders even designate *Thinking Rooms* —creative concentration centers—where staff can escape the rigors of the workday and focus their thoughts.

Think of these *Thinking Rooms* the way Winnie the Pooh regarded his *Thoughtful Spot:* a haven to concentrate with all the vigor of Auguste Rodin's famous 7-foot tall bronze sculpture *The Thinker.* Thinking Rooms have even been designed for sports teams. In professional basketball for example, the Chicago Bulls had a sanctuary for their thinking—a place where they could go to get away from the screams of the fans, the whistles of the officials, the chastising of the coaches and the carping of the media. Phil Jackson, who coached the Bulls to six NBA Championship seasons, designated and designed the team's Thinking *Room.* For players only. No coaches. No management. The walls were festooned with Native American artifacts that stimulated thinking. A wood arrow with a tobacco pouch — a symbol of prayer—hung on one wall. Another wall displayed a bear claw necklace—a symbol of power. In this space, players could parlay their thoughts on their individual and collective performances—past, present and future—without any repercussions from each other and without any criticism from management.

Leaders leverage the value in a venue.

They know that the design of a space can spice the behavioral accent of the place. Consider the barbershop designed as if were a baseball field. The waiting area looks like a dugout. The barber's chair is located at home plate so the men and boys waiting to get their hair cut can fantasize hitting the home run or game-winning hit. The dugout design heightens behavioral expectations. That's why leaders also design and designate various other rooms to stimulate expected behavior. Consider the:

- Briefing Room
- Card Room
- Chat Room
- Control Room
- Dressing Room
- Emergency Room
- Game Room
- Living Room
- Sewing Room
- Waiting Room

Why not a *Thinking Room*? Think of it as a room for improvement furnished of course with those proverbial blankets that keeps your team secure, confident and productive.

Today's ImproveMINT

Designate a Team Inter-Sanctum
to keep your leadership thinking in mint condition.

Mint 98

Tilling The Soil
To Grow Your Ideas

Reading time: 3:18

Hopping in the car, the two executives rambled down the country road lined with corn fields that had just been tilled and planted. Linda, the passenger says: "Hey, Diane, congrats on getting that speaking opportunity at the convention next week. How's your speech coming along?" The driver says: "Okay, I reviewed it with my speechwriter the other day. But I really don't have time to rehearse it. Just too busy." Her passenger acknowledges how busy everyone is, especially these two executives. "Yeah, I hear ya'. Busy. Yeah, who's got time to rehearse anyway," Linda opined as the rows of corn fields whizzed by. And then she added, "Just look at all those rows of corn. I'm sure glad that farmer rehearsed."

Now Diane, the driver is confused. How does a farmer rehearse planting corn? And who cares? Linda, her passenger clarifies: "Well, I love popcorn and a good movie and corn on the cob on the grill and if that farmer didn't rehearse there would be less popcorn in the world." Huh? Now Diane is really confused.

But then Linda explained the literal meaning of the word —REHEARSAL. It stems from the Middle English word that means to dig the earth, to hoe a row, to harrow. Over and over again. Clearing away the clutter. The farmer tills the soil so that the seeds can take root and grow. Linda further explained that a written speech is like so many seeds that the speaker/writer has stacked up page by page to feed to the audience. The key is making sure those ideas stick in the minds of your audience and take root in their heart and souls so that your seeds grow to fruition in the audience's memory long after you have climbed down from your tractor—the podium—after attempting to plant your seeds in THEIR fields. Diane was intrigued. "So what you're saying is that I have to really STICK it to the audience," the driver said with a grin. Her passenger retorted: "Well that's a lot more effective than just trying to shovel it at 'em. Especially you. I know you too well. Your audience will need some big boots." The two friends laughed together. Then they reminded each other of speakers who were famous for "sticking it to the audience"—for rehearsing. They mentioned for example that Winston Churchill rehearsed his speeches aloud while standing on the bow of a ship. Then the two executives laughed in recalling the story they heard at a convention when a speaker obviously did not rehearse his speech.

"We Built the Largest Condom-"

That day he lost more than eye contact with his audience. He also lost his credibility. He absent-mindedly read the last word on a page, realizing too late that it was a hyphenated word that continued on the next page. He was supposed to read, "We built the largest condominium in the city." Instead the audience heard, "We built the largest CONDOM." The audience smirked when the speaker let his script so embarrassingly show. And instead of "sticking it" to the audience, he stuck himself with his foot firmly wedged in his mouth and his cheeks flushed with embarrassment. The two executives laughed at that story and then the driver pulled into a convenience store. "Hey Linda, I need to get a bag of popcorn," Diane said. "I'll munch on it after rehearsing my speech tonight. "Oh, I thought you were too busy," Linda chided. Diane retorted: "Oh, no, never too busy to stick it—and make it stick!

Today's ImproveMINT

Rehearse your speeches
to keep your leadership thinking in mint condition.

●

Mint 99

Billiiiiooooooonnnnnsss Tuning In Your Tone

Reading time: 3:48

Mark Twain, the famous author and humorist put on a shirt. It had a missing button. He put on another shirt. It had a missing button. He put on a third shirt. It, too, had a missing button. Twain then unleashed a swirl of swear words. His wife, standing right behind him, heard every expletive. Then she methodically repeated every profane word back to him in hopes of embarrassing her husband. But Twain took it all in and then looked deep into the eyes of his wife and deadpanned: "You have the words, but not the music." The most effective leaders have both the words and the music in their voices and both the content and the tone in their hearts tuned to commanding the moment at hand— somber and staid or celebratory and triumphant. No one could ever forget the way scientist and author Carl Sagan spoke of: *"Billlliooooooonnnnnnnnss & Billlliooooooonnnnnnnsss of stars!"* The turbulence in his voice articulated the vastness of the universe. The trembling whisper in his vocal cords vibrated like so many musical chords soaring through light years of awe, wonder and mystery. And the rumbling of his voice rambled through the void of space.

Leaders know they can use more than their voices to stir the imaginations of others with Sound Sensations that can ignite fear and furor with something more than a scream, something more than nails scratching on a slate board and something more right at the tips of your fingers. A senator in the United States opened a news conference with some Sound Sensations from his fingers. No words. Just 56 knocks on a table over 81 seconds. In a rhythmic beat. Each blow corresponding to each of the 56 blows that Rodney King suffered in 81 seconds at the hands of the Los Angeles police in 1992. The senator –Bill Bradley of New Jersey - let his fists at his fingertips do the talking. The Senator's attention-commanding communication underscores a significant leadership skill: *"Leaders don't settle for making a speech. They orchestrate a message."* Opera audiences have long experienced the power in understanding the tone more than the tune. No one in the audience missed a beat when a last minute fill-in at the Metropolitan Opera House in New York City forgot the words of an aria. With passion and great deal of poise, the understudy opera singer simply sang the title of the opera—*La Traviata*—over and over again. He sang it so passionately and poignantly in a stirring tone that the audience gave him a standing ovation.

Tone is a critical element to engage others. Leaders tune in to their audiences with just the right tone. Roman orators even commissioned a flute player to keep them in tune. Whenever the orator's voice began to rise in pitch and therefore lower in its authoritarian tone, a flute player would play a low note to signal the speaker to lower his voice. When a speaker tunes to an audience, the speaker feels what the audience feels. These sympathetic vibrations set a tone that has the audience virtually humming along, adding depth and meaning to the leader's words with a pitch that engages the audience to follow the leader wherever you go as if you were the Podium Pied Piper. The leadership lesson is clear: before you make your pitch— pitch your tone.

Today's ImproveMINT

Use vocal variety in your speech
to keep your leadership thinking in mint condition.

Mint 100

Kissing Sleeping Beauty Or Prince Charming

Reading time: 3:27

Wake up your audience. That should be your objective as soon as you begin your speech. Think of your audience as Sleeping Beauty or Prince Charming (or your Sleeping Significant Other) locked in a 100-year deep sleep. Your mission: AWAKEN your audience to your point of view. Open your audience's eyes with this proverbial kiss: a 7-step process to structure your next speech that begins with Wake Up and ends with Wind Up.

1. WAKE UP:

TEASE your audience. TEASE is an acrostic for 5 compelling ways to begin your speech:

- (*Testimonial*)   Reference an expert to add credibility.
- (*Example*)   Provide specifics from history.
- (*Anecdote*)   Tell stories from biographies/ experiences.
- (*Statement*)   Create a catch-phrase
  to establish an arresting opening.
- (*Evidence*)   Provide third-party for credibility.

2. WARM UP:

Reach out and let the audience know you are just like them. Show them you care about them and they will care even more about you. They will listen more actively and engage their minds with yours. They will follow your lead.

3. WHAT'S UP:

Tell the audience what this speech is about. Billboard the essence of your message in 10 words or less. Write a headline that embodies the theme of your message, sets the tone and foreshadows the conclusion. Use this headline to anchor your point of view. Develop this headline as a mantra the audience can follow to better understand, assimilate and act on your message.

4. WHIP UP:

Tune in to the needs of the audience. Boldly answer their question: What's in it for me? Spark their enthusiasm. Flame their fears of what would happen if they don't listen. Show them how your ideas will be meaningful to them because your thinking is in tune with their thinking. See *Tuning In to WII-FM (What's in it for me)* page 199, Mint 76.

5. WELL UP:

Use personal stories and humor to flesh out your message with an emotional appeal. Facts tell but stories sell. Sell your message by increasing its PH count — P for personal stories and H for humor. (See stories, page 25, Mint 5)

6. WRAP UP:

As you conclude, restate the headline (see What's Up) and summarize the highlights of your speech.

7. WIND UP:

Close your speech with a strong call to action that confirms your intent, commands your purpose and commits your audience to feel, think or do.

Today's ImproveMINT
***First wake up your audience
to keep your leadership thinking in mint condition***

●

Mint 101

Speak Up
Join Toastmasters

Reading time: 6:55

Your palms are moist. Your mouth is dry. Your stomach is churning. Your eyes are burning. And your lips are quivering. You're sure you're going to die just as soon as you step up to that podium. Your discomfort is normal, especially for infrequent or inexperienced public speakers. So is your fear. As Joshua Liebman writes in his book *Peace of Mind*: "If we were to take away man's capacity to fear, we would take away also his capacity to grow since fear is often a stimulus to growth, the goad to invention." Properly channeled, fear can become a catalyst for your growth as a leader in general and public speaker in particular. Your fear can heighten your awareness, energize your body language and focus your concentration.

Likewise the most effective leaders realize that fear (a.k.a. stage fright) comes with the territory. As author and public speaker Mark Twain once observed: "There are two types of speakers: those that are nervous and those that are liars." The most effective leaders understand that fear is your body's calling card, summoning up just the right amount of adrenalin to prod and provoke you beyond your comfort zone so that you can stand before more than one other person and speak your mind. Most first time and infrequent speakers see the DANGER signs posted all around the podium: *"Keep Out: Warning. Warning. The Fear of Public Speaking is the #1 fear of most people."* In fact, Public Speaking is a fear greater than the fear of death or snakes, according to the *Book of Lists*. That fear is exacerbated when they learn that the fear of public speaking can even afflict the brave like astronaut Gus Grissom: "Asking Gus to just say a few words was like handing him a knife and asking him to open a main vein," writes author Tom Wolfe in *The Right Stuff*. Grissom commanded the first Gemini manned space flight and logged more than 100 missions as a fighter pilot during the Korean Conflict yet he suffered podium-itis.

The fear of public speaking can also afflict the powerful. Winston Churchill, the Prime Minister of Great Britain during World War II, said he became so nervous before speaking in public he felt like a nine-inch brick of ice hit him in the stomach. And when you're that nervous you pollute your speeches with an array of verbal tics from a flood of Ums and Errrs to punctuating every other sentence with "you know." You know. Yes we know. Consider Caroline ("you know") Kennedy. The daughter of President John Kennedy crashed her senatorial aspiration into a wall of "you knows" and "ums" before her ill-fated maiden run for public office even began in 2009. Caroline Kennedy's bout with the microphone is personal proof that effective public speaking is a learned skill not an inherited trait. That's the good news. And that means, no matter how much you dread public speaking, you can learn how to speak up with confidence in public. You can stifle those Ums and Errrs. You can bury those "you knows." How? Seek refuge. Join Toastmasters International, an organization with 14,350 clubs in 122 countries (at this writing in 2014). They meet weekly and you can learn and participate at your own pace.

A Thank You to Toastmasters

The author of **Leadership Mints** has 15 years of experience in Toastmasters to thank for stimulating him to research and write this book. Many of these Leadership Mints were first developed as speeches for his fellow Toastmasters. In fact The Leadership Mints Guy, Peter Jeff wrote his first book on goal-setting **(Get a GRIP on Your Dream,** ISBN 0-938716-63-8, PossibilityPress.com) based on the research he first did in writing and delivering a series of speeches for Toastmasters on **G**oal-setting, **R**isk-Making, **I**nitiating and **P**ersisting – or GRIP for short.

Turning Your Fears
Into Cheers

Toastmasters International has a 90-year-plus history as the world's largest organization (292,000 members) helping ordinary adults (18 and over) from all walks of life enhance their public speaking and personal leadership skills. Each member of the club assumes various leadership roles and speaking opportunities on a voluntary basis. Members meet weekly to learn communications and leadership skills at their own pace. There are no mandatory meetings. Visit a Toastmasters club near you. It's free for visitors and only $36 for 6-months if you decide to join.

And relax, you don't have to speak if you don't want to in the first few meetings. Just watch how others are turning their fears into cheers at the podium or lectern. Practice your public speaking and leading skills each week at Toastmasters meetings. Get helpful feedback and support from your fellow Toastmasters. Your peers will provide you on-going encouragement and support and you will learn tips and techniques to try to continuously improve your public speaking skills. That feedback at Toastmasters meetings helped to sharpen the author's teaching effectiveness as a college adjunct public speaking instructor for 10 years. And his Toastmasters experience certainly enhanced his professionalism in coaching executives to develop their own podium prowess. But most of all Toastmasters helped the author of this book develop and practice leadership skills from treating others with dignity and respect to providing meaningful and constructive feedback that stimulated others to actively listen and learn from criticism and on- going coaching and feedback. When you visit a Toastmasters meeting you will see others like you facing the challenge of becoming a more persuasive and confident public speaker. You will see Toastmasters of various ages and stages in their careers. And you will learn from all of them. At least that's been this author's personal experience. To find a Toastmasters Club near you: Call 1.949.858.8255. Or visit (www.toastmasters. org).

About
Toastmasters International

From Toastmasters.org

Toastmasters International is a non-profit educational organization that teaches public speaking and leadership skills through a worldwide network of meeting locations. Headquartered in Rancho Santa Margarita, California, the organization has more than 292,000 memberships in more than 14,350 clubs in 122 countries.

Making an Investment
In Yourself

From Toastmasters.org

A Toastmasters meeting is a learn-by-doing workshop in which participants hone their speaking and leadership skills in a no-pressure atmosphere. There is no instructor in a Toastmasters meeting. Instead, members evaluate one another's presentations. This feedback process is a key part of the program's success. Meeting participants also give impromptu talks on assigned topics, conduct meetings and develop skills related to timekeeping, grammar and parliamentary procedure.

Members learn communication skills by working in the Competent Communications Manual, a series of 10 self-paced speaking assignments designed to instill a basic foundation in public speaking. Membership in Toastmasters is one of the greatest investments you can make in yourself. At $36 every six months (club dues may vary), it is also one of the most cost-effective skill-building tools available anywhere.

Today's ImproveMINT

Practice Public Speaking with Toastmasters
to keep your leadership thinking in mint condition.

●

COMMUNICATING

Leadership Mints
Extra Bonus

See next page for real world examples
of communications leadership at the podium.

Ending Your Speech With Pizzazz

Reading time: 4:46

Thank You! Those two words, powerful on the lips of every effective leader at the end of a project, are powerless at the end of a speech. That's why the most effective leaders find a more powerful, more productive and more permeating way to conclude a speech. They drive toward their conclusion in high gear—with an attitude! Not a platitude—albeit politicians who can't resist blessing America.   It is instructive to note that of the 217 speeches listed in William Safire's anthology: *Lend Me Your Ears: Great Speeches in History,* only seven conclude with "Thank you." Indeed, effective speakers leave their audiences thinking the way effective comedians leave their audiences laughing. If you were concluding a speech on the importance of embracing change, you could refer to an historical figure like Abraham Lincoln and end on a quote:

> *Our tomorrows need new and different solutions today. We have to recall the insight of President Abraham Lincoln on the brink of the Civil War. Lincoln said, "The dogmas of the quiet past are inadequate for the stormy present and future, as our circumstances are new, we must think anew and act anew."*

You can also use the cadence in your voice to shift your conclusion into a higher gear and rhythmically bring the audience along with repeated phrasing that builds to a climax and makes a "thank you" seem even more superfluous. Your voice booms with an energy and an enthusiasm. Then your voice fades into a stark silence that ironically seems to scream your message even louder and bolder. You look directly into the eyes of one member of the audience and you count to yourself 1,001, 1,002, 1,003. Then you chant your cadence in delivering these words to conclude your speech in a more stirring manner than your basic "thank you."

> *"And so what we have been saying in*
> *the words of that famous writer,*
> *Mr. or Mrs. Anonymous, that life is an*
> *adventure:*
> *"Dare it. A duty, perform it.*
> *An opportunity, take it.*
> *A journey, complete it.*
> *A promise, fulfill it.*
> *A puzzle, solve it.*
> *A goal, achieve it."*

Let that last phrase — "achieve it" —sink into the minds and hearts of the audience. Then you step away from the podium and bow your head. The audience will see your cue and start to applaud. If you simply can't wait for the audience applause, fight the urge to say "thank you." Instead say: "Now let me hear from you. Who has the first question?" If the audience is still reticent you ask yourself the first question to prime the audience pump. "One question that seems to be on the minds of many people I talk to about this is......"

15 Ways To End Your Speech Beyond Thank You

Here are 15 other ways that you can end a speech effectively without resorting to the well-worn, thank you. These key phrases are like highway signposts—markers that tell the audience it's time for you to exit the highway of ideas you've been driving down, markers that tell the audience it's time for them to hop in the driver's seat and take your message even further down the road.

1. **Appreciative:**   And so let me applaud you for what you have done.

2. **Benediction**:   May you stay healthy and wise.
3. **Challenge:**   In closing, I challenge you to....
4. **Circular:**   So we arrive at where we began and I trust that...
5. **Expectation:**   I   look   forward   to...

6. **Interrogative:**   Let me conclude with this question.
7. **Invitation:**   Join us and know that together we can make the world a better place.
8. **Preemptory:**   As I close, let me ask myself the first question.
9. **Proverbial:**   May the transformational force be with you.
10. **Ritual:**   And so in closing we end the book on this chapter and look forward to beginning the next book with you.

11. **Salutation:**   I   salute   you   and   your organization for...
12. **Sing Song:**   So let me hear it one more time, what should we do? (audience response)
13. **Solicitation:**   And so let me conclude by asking you for your help.
14. **Suggestive:**   Before I take your questions, let me close with this thought.
15. **Summation:**   And so what we have been discussing here today is...

Now   let's   use   that   last   technique—the summation—to end this Extra Bonus Leadership Mint on ending your speech with pizzazz. *"And so you have 15 ways to end your speech with a bang in a way that your audiences will more fully remember and more fully act on your words. Use one of those effective closings and chances are your audiences will Thank YOU."*

AFTERWARD

NOW is the Time
Reading time: 2:19

4-year-old daughter:	"Dad, what time is it?"
Dad:	"Now."
4-year-old daughter:	"Yeah, now."
Dad:	"Now."
4-year-old daughter:	"Stop fooling around, dad. What time is it?
Dad:	"Now. Now is the only time that really matters.

In the NOW, leaders know that yesterday is a cancelled check; tomorrow a promissory note. Today is the only real currency leaders have to spend. In the Now, leaders leverage the moment into MOMENTum! In the Now, leaders see more congruence than coincidence in the quirk that the word "Now "is "Won" spelled backwards. And in the Now, leaders come to more readily kNOW. Yet too many still procrastinate. They're paralyzed in their own fear. They're frozen in their own time. They're stuck waiting for that NEXT station in life.

You know that NEXT station where you'll FINALLY achieve your dreams after the kids are out of college, or FINALLY get that promotion after the owner retires, or FINALLY win that piece of business after your new product introduction, or FINALLY buy that bigger house after you get that bonus. Stop waiting. Act NOW. "Relish the moment" as poet Robert J. Hastings urges in his poem *The Station*: Now

Is The Best Time of Your Life. As Hastings observes what really drives us crazy "is the regret over yesterday and the fear of tomorrow. Regret and fear are twin thieves that rob us of today."

NOW is the time to rise above regret and fear. That's why they call The Present a gift as Ziggy says. No wonder a good plan executed NOW is far better than a perfect plan executed next week as General George Patton noted.

- Act NOW on your investment in **LEADERSHIP MINTS.**

- Act NOW on applying the ImproveMINTS in these 101 Leadership Mints.

- Act NOW on the inherent potency you have in your hands right now as you reflect on the following inscription that marks a prominent sundial:

"The shadow by my finger cast
Divides the future from the past.

"Behind its unreturning line,
The vanished hour no longer thine.

"Before it lies the unknown hour
In darkness and beyond thine power.

"One hour alone is in thine hands,
The now on which the shadow stands."

EPILOG

Dispensing Your
101 Leadership Mints
As Easy As 1-2-3

Reading time: 2:51

Now that you have sampled all 101 **Leadership Mints,** here's a way to repackage your Mints with PEZ-like ease for quick access when you need to freshen your feeling for leading. Linking PEZ— the flavored tiny bricks of candy—to after-dinner mints is not as farfetched as it seems. After all PEZ—first marketed as a breath mint for adults in 1927— owes its iconic name to the first, middle and last letters of the German word for peppermint –**P**feff**E**rmin**Z.** Just as the sequence of letters was key to the formation of PEZ as a brand, so too is the sequence you follow in accessing your 101 Leadership Mints. It's as easy as 1-2-3 to fashion your own PEZ-like dispenser for easy and quick access to your Leadership Mints and freshen your feeling for leading. Just follow this 1-2-3 sequence in retrieving your Mints: 1. Creativity, 2. Collaboration , 3. Communications.

- ONE: Start with a continuous improvement mindset (creativity).
- TWO: then link up with helping hands (collaboration) and
- THREE: only then share your message (communication). It's as easy as 1-2-3.

Then apply that easy-as-1-2-3 approach to reviewing the first three mints that lead off each of three sections of the book (Creativity, Collaboration and Communications) to readily access your 101 Leadership Mints with PEZ-like ease.

1. CREATIVITY

In reviewing the first three mints in Part I of the **Leadership Mints** book on Creativity, (ONE) remind yourself to reconnect with a mentor, a colleague, a friend to serve as your sounding board   (Mint 1) and (TWO) then make the time to think and meditate for a few minutes every day (Mint 2) on what's important and why. Then (THREE) look for solutions to complex problems that are clear and simple (Mint 3). The most effective leaders step back to first assess the situation long before rushing out to take command of the situation.

2. COLLABORATION

In reviewing the first three mints in Part II of the **Leadership Mints** book on Collaborating, remind yourself to (ONE) allocate your full attention and concentration (Mint 35) on another person —a colleague, a superior, or a direct report. (TWO) Commit your full support (Mint 36) and (THREE) be aware of the feelings and expectations of others (Mint 37).

3. COMMUNICATION

In reviewing the first three mints in Part III of the **Leadership Mints** on Communicating, focus (ONE) first on listening for clarity and understanding (Mint 67), (TWO) heighten your attention span to discern the viability of what's specifically you are listening to (Mint 68) and (THREE) communicate with your eyes long before your voice (Mint 69). Then scan the list of 101 ImproveMINTS on the Addendum beginning on the next page.

ImproveMINTS

(In chronological order Mints 1 to 101)

Mint 1   Establish a Sounding Board.

Mint 2   Meditation.

Mint 3   Simplify.

Mint 4   Emphasize the purpose and dignity of work.

Mint 5   Share your personal stories

Mint 6   Leverage your sense of perspective.

Mint 7   Be inquisitive.

Mint 8   Reframe an issue to better cope.

Mint 9   Creatively tap in to hidden resources.

Mint 10   Find inspiration in children's books.

Mint 11   Get out of your office/ workplace run away.

Mint 12   Ride the RODEO of creativity.

Mint 13   Creatively use your existing resources.

Mint 14   Look for substitute resources.

Mint 15   Break out of your Perception Prison.

Mint 16   Be aware of other points of view.

Mint 17   Laugh at yourself.

Mint 18   Hone your sense of humor.

Mint 19   Stay vigilant reviewing familiar information.

Mint 20   Dust off the cobwebs in your brain.

Mint 21   Supersize your leadership

Mint 22   Keep looking for chinks in your own armor.

Mint 23   Think strategically and consequentially.

Mint 24   Appreciate the awesome power of your brain.

Mint 25   Rein in your impulsive thinking.

Mint 26   Narrow your focus.

Mint 27   Turn devastation into a fresh start.

Mint 28   Cleanse Your Thinking.

Mint 29   Climb up to new heights.

Mint 30   Repurpose your resources.

Mint 31   Sing a song at least in your heart.

Mint 32   Visually post all brainstorming ideas.

Mint 33   Clear away the clutter in your mind.

Mint 34   Accelerate quickly out of the blocks.

Mint 35   Concentrate fully.

Mint 36   Love and respect your staff /teammates.

Mint 37   Express your feelings.

Mint 38   Respect all, even those who disrespect you.

Mint 39   Stay connected to others.

Mint 40   Seek compatibility first in persuading others.

Mint 41   DESIGNate more than deleGATE.

Mint 42   Align your staff's talents and skills.

Mint 43   Embrace your staff.

Mint 44   Rely on each other.

Mint 45   Seek complementary relationships.

Mint 46   Validate the situation others are facing.

Mint 47   Serve your employee's needs first.

Mint 48   Collaborate informally AFTER a project.

Mint 49   Credit the value of all partners.

Mint 50   Foster faith in others.

Mint 51   Value your vulnerability.
Mint 52   Get to know your staff personally.
Mint 53   Trust others first to earn their trust.
Mint 54   Hone your humility.
Mint 55   Keep an open mind. Say AND not BUT.
Mint 56   Serving without undermining another.
Mint 57   Value your introverted leaders.
Mint 58   Adapt to other personality styles.
Mint 59   Express your need for interaction.
Mint 60   Be specific in praising others.

Mint 61   Keep your ego in check.
Mint 62   Embrace criticism
Mint 63   Leverage your self-control.
Mint 64   Reprimand with emotional intelligence.
Mint 65   Pump LIFE into your proposals.
Mint 66   Stay in touch with the rank and file.
Mint 67   Guard against jumping to conclusions.
Mint 68   Sharpen your listening skills.
Mint 69   Speak with your eyes.
Mint 70   Make LOVE *(Look on Vitally Engaged)*.

Mint 71   FLIRT with your audience.
Mint 72   Increase your face value with a smile.
Mint 73   Your body speaks louder than you do.
Mint 74   Think long and slowly over time.
Mint 75   Flow into the ideas of others.

Mint 76   Tune in to the interests of your audience.

Mint 77   Embrace change boldly & visually.

Mint 78   Use analogy to explain complex issues.

Mint 79   Master the magic of the metaphor.

Mint 80   Generate positive nicknames for your staff.

Mint 81   Visually connect with your audience.

Mint 82   Beware of looking too polished.

Mint 83   Vary your pace in speaking publicly.

Mint 84   Parlay the power of the paradox.

Mint 85   Leverage your message visually.

Mint 86   Value the energizing nature of change.

Mint 87   Revise and rewrite often.

Mint 88   Write a preSCRIPTion for your audience.

Mint 89   Edit yourself before you speak or write.

Mint 90   Use your writing skill as a problem-solving tool.

Mint 91   Take your business cards personally.

Mint 92   Apologize in writing and in person.

Mint 93   Write a 5:15 update every Friday afternoon.

Mint 94   Master the role of master of ceremonies.

Mint 95   Give presenters enthusiastic introductions.

Mint 96   Include a Premise in an agenda.

Mint 97   Designate a Team Inter-Sanctum.

Mint 98   Rehearse your speeches.

Mint 99   Use vocal variety in your speech.

Mint 100   First wake up your audience.

Mint 101   Practice public speaking with Toastmasters.

Overview

By Leadership Behaviors & Mint #

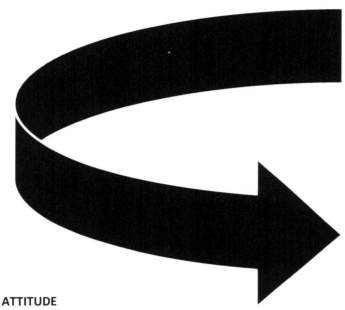

ATTITUDE

Mint 21   Height Insight: Attitude More Than Altitude
Mint 31   Whistle While You Work
Mint 33   Firing Up Your Personal Zamboni
Mint 41   Becoming the Chairman of the Bored
Mint 63   Self-Control The Ultimate Power

BODY LANGUAGE

Mint 72   Smiling to Leverage Your Face Value
Mint 73   Arming Yourself With Body Language

CONFLICT MANAGEMENT

Mint 55   Get Off Your Buts
Mint 64   SCORE Don't Get Sore
Mint 65   Throw 'em a LIFE Line

INNOVATION

MEETINGS

PERCEPTION

PUBLIC SPEAKING

RELATIONSHIP BUILDING

STRATEGIC THINKING

TEAMWORK

WRITING

CONTENTS

Mint 1-101 Chronologically

Part I

CREATING

Part II

COLLABORATING

Part III
COMMUNICATING

PERSONAL BONUS MINT

Preview Your Next 90 Days

Race horses explode out of the starting gate and head for the first turn: 16 horses jockeying for position. What if your leadership skills were like those 16 different horses in the starting gate, each jockeying for position? And what if you thought of your next annual review as if it were the finish line in a one-mile race? By the quarter-mile mark (in 90 days), you would have a pretty good idea just how skillfully you are leading all 16 different horses or just how woefully you are just along for the ride. But of course your chances of winning the race, of performing well through the remaining 3/4 of a mile — throughout the remaining 9 months of completing your annual review —will depend on how well you anticipate and compensate for challenges ahead to your leadership skills and your ability to shore up your weaknesses and affirm your strengths literally on the run — in the heat of battle— and against vigorous countervailing interests.

That's why the most effective leaders conduct a QUARTERLY PREVIEW — more than simply an annual review —in evaluating their staffs' skills on the job. Career Development then becomes a visionary process--an on-going race to a non-existent finish line-- more than a punitive report card on a random calendar date 12 months away. (And how many "annual" reviews are conducted 3-6 months late? Too many.) Small wonder the word — "career"—stems from the French word for a race course. In this proverbial career race, the "victory" goes to the jockey who can best keep track of all 16 of his or her horses at the same time over time. And much like a horse race fan, the leader in you sizes up your 16 different horses (i.e. traits) with a predictive eye toward continuous overall improvement long-term and a winning performance short-term. The focus is always ahead—the next 90 days, the next quarter in PREVIEWING what could be -- not simply reviewing what has been. And like a seasoned jockey, you as the leader continuously leverage your strengths and compensate for your weaknesses. You anticipate challenges ahead and stay focused on a productive performance especially in adverse conditions. You adapt and adjust. That's why the most effective leaders line up their career development skills -- their horses in the starting gate -- according to a specific set of leadership skills. Let's use John Zenger 's list of 16 leadership traits as he delineated in the *Harvard Business Review.* In alphabetical order:

1. Change Champion
2. Communicates powerfully
3. Develops others
4. Initiates
5. Innovates
6. Inspires
7. Integrity
8. Problem Solver
9. Results focused
10. Self-Development
11. Stretch Goals
12. Relationship Builder
13. Teamwork
14. Technical Expertise
15. Strategic Perspective
16. Relevancy (to the outside world).

Now put these 16 horses in the gate. Handicap them 1-16. The No. 1 horse is your strongest trait. The No. 16 horse is your weakest trait. Size up your race every 90 days. Are you still in the race or have you gotten off track? Compare how well you are performing over time to achieve the following desired behaviors:

1. Shows concern for others.
2. Acts in the team's best interests.
3. Acts independently.
4. Seeks challenges.
5. Learns from failure/success.
6. Listens, provides feedback.
7. Personally accountable.
8. Quick to act.
9. Challenges the status quo.
10. Deals well with ambiguity.
11. Anticipates problems.
12. Involves others.
13. Connects emotionally with others.
14. Develops others.
15. Customer-focused.
16. Practices diversity.

Index Leadership Mints

How to Lead a 5-Minute Leadership Mints Break

FOR BUSY LEADERS
DEVELOPING OTHER LEADERS

Take 5 minutes during your staff meetings on a regular basis to enjoy a 5-Minute Leadership Mints Break based on the 101 stories personalizing values-based leadership principles in this book by The Leadership Mints Guy (Peter Jeff):

LEADERSHIP MINTS
101 Ways to Freshen
Your Feeling For Leading

Recharge, rewind, and remind yourself of your values-based leadership principles while helping to develop other busy leaders quickly and easily—like digesting a candy mint and just as invigorating. Savor a Leadership Mint—a meaningful and memorable short story on exemplary leadership behavior that provides:

- EngageMINT that takes less than five minutes to read.
- AlignMINT that more fully focuses your leadership skills in one of 16 different competencies.
- ImproveMINT, a one-line summary of the key leadership learning at the end of each Leadership Mint for your continued Professional DevelopMINT.

Here's how you conduct a 5-minute Leadership Mints Break during a staff meeting:

1. A staff member is chosen the week before to

lead the *5-Minute Leadership Mints Break* at the next staff meeting.

2. That designated Leadership Mints Break Leader assigns the MINT story (out of the 101 available) to be read prior to the next staff meeting.

3. At the next staff meeting the Leadership Mints Break Leader then leads a discussion on the leadership principle called out in that assigned Mint (story). Fun option: Pass around a candy dish of wrapped mints for all to enjoy while savoring their Leadership Mints.

With their own personal hard copy of **Leadership Mints**, staffers might display the book like a mint candy dish on their desk/work area throughout the week. With that on-going visual reminder – of a refreshing walk along a nature trail beneath the canopy of leafy trees-- staffers will more readily reinforce the refreshing and reinvigorating value of the **Leadership Mints** learning and leading experience. Then staffers might increase their leadership improveMINTS with more just-in-time reading. Indeed, with the book at their fingers tips and the reading time for each Leadership Mint printed just below its headline, staffers might leverage their sporadic reading opportunities throughout their busy day and reinforce the book's founding concept: *Invest a few minutes reading for a lifetime of leading.*

See page 242
Use the Meeting POP template to arrange your first 5-minute Leadership Mints Break.

About the Author

Peter Jeff is a leadership development consultant, coach, and founder of the leadership blog that spawned this book (LeadershipMints.com). He is also the author of a personal leadership book on goal-setting published by Possibility Press:

Get a GRIP on Your Dream,
12 Ways to Squeeze
More Success Out of Your Goals
ISBN 0-938716-63-8

Known as The *Leadership Mints Guy,* Mr. Jeff held a ringside seat in the Executive Suite for more than 25 years. As a corporate affairs leader, he consulted with executive management on a range of leadership issues from conflict management to employee engagement. Contact:

E-mail LeadershipMintsGuy@gmail.com
Tweet (@LeaderMintsGuy
Visit: www.LeadershipMints.com

●

Purchase additional copies of:

LEADERSHIP MINTS
101 Ways to Freshen Your Feeling for Leading

at Amazon.com

Made in the USA
Charleston, SC
13 March 2015